Ancient Peoples and Places

SOUTH WEST ENGLAND

General Editor

DR. GLYN DANIEL

ABOUT THE AUTHOR

After working for the British School at Rome 1929–30, and undergoing excavation training at Richborough, Kent and Hembury, Devon, Aileen Henderson married Cyril (now Sir Cyril) Fox, the then director of the National Museum of Wales, Cardiff, in 1933. Between 1936 and 1946 she took part in numerous excavations in England and Wales, often accompanying her husband. From 1940 to 1946 she was Lecturer in Archaeology at University College, Cardiff. Since 1947 she has been Lecturer in British Archaeology at the University College of the South West, now Exeter University.

Lady Fox has done much field research on Dartmooor, at Roman sites in Devon, on hill-forts, etc. She has served on the Council of the Prehistoric Society and other similar bodies. Her main interests are the Iron Age and Roman periods in Britain.

Ancient Peoples and Places

SOUTH WEST ENGLAND

Aileen Fox

98 PHOTOGRAPHS
36 LINE DRAWINGS
15 MAPS

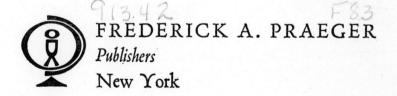

FREDERICK A. PRAEGER
Publishers
New York

THIS IS VOLUME FORTY–ONE IN THE SERIES

Ancient Peoples and Places

GENERAL EDITOR: DR. GLYN DANIEL

BOOKS THAT MATTER
Published in the United States of America
in 1964 by Frederick A. Praeger, Inc.,
Publisher, 111 Fourth Ave.,
New York 3, N.Y.
Library of Congress Catalog Card Number: 64–17678
Printed in Holland

CONTENTS

5

ILLUSTRATIONS

8

9

Foreword

I HAVE LONG WANTED to write a book about the Archaeology of South-West England, in which it would be possible
to consider the early human settlement of the peninsula as a
whole and to forget about county boundaries. I am deeply
grateful to the Editor, Dr Glyn Daniel, for suggesting that it
should be included in this series and for waiting until I was
free to write it. I am conscious now of its imperfections, realising
that with the increasing flow of new discoveries, excavations
and the re-assessment of old material, it is almost impossible to
get everything correctly focussed in the short compass of this
volume. I have been enabled to make this attempt by the kindness of many friends and fellow-workers who have discussed the
various problems and who have given me information in advance of publication: I am particularly indebted in this way to
Arthur ApSimon, Professor J. D. Evans, Peter Fowler, C. A.
Ralegh Radford, Andrew Saunders, Charles Thomas,
Bernard Wailes, and Dr F. S. Wallis. In addition I have
benefited from the informed criticism of Leo Rivet in Chapters
7 and 8 and from advice from C. E. Stevens in Chapter 9.

For assistance with the illustrations I am much indebted to
my former students Gillian Lamacraft (Mrs Mitchell) and
Christine Wilkins, as well as Mr R. Fry and Miss R. Bethell,
technicians in the Department of Geography and Mr W.
Hoskin, the University photographer. I should also like to
acknowledge with gratitude the helpful cooperation of the
curators of the museums at Exeter, Taunton and Truro
in placing objects at our disposal for photography, and also the
kindness of Mr Charles Wolfe of Newquay in allowing me to
select photographs of sites from his collection. The final form
of the maps I owe to the skill of Mr. H. A. Shelley.   A. F.

CHAPTER I

The Place

THE SEA IS NEVER FAR AWAY in the south-west; even on the high moorlands, on Dartmoor and Bodmin, there is a gleam on the horizon and nearing the Atlantic coast the windswept land flattens, the colours in the landscape brighten and the character of the peninsula asserts itself. Lying with its long axis east and west, it extends on the north from Bridge-water Bay and on the south from Lyme Regis Bay to the granite cliffs of Land's End, a distance of approximately 130 miles: at its widest, from Prawle Point, Salcombe to the Foreland at Lynton, it is about 75 miles across, narrowing to some 20 miles from Padstow to St Austell westwards. The western coast faces the Atlantic which pounds at a line of sheer cliffs from Land's End to Morte Point, the northern fronts the Bristol Channel looking across to South Wales, whilst the south coast, which is more indented, is at the end of the English Channel as it widens to meet the ocean. Ringed by salt water in this way, the peninsula has received sea-borne immigrants from varied sources in prehistoric times and its inhabitants have established a wide range of overseas trading contacts, particularly with the continental Atlantic coasts.

Geographically it is somewhat set apart from the rest of England, not only by the surrounding seas but by a large area of fen and marsh, the Somerset Levels, which extend from the foot of the Mendip hills to the Quantocks and for over 20 miles inland. Consequently there is a tendency for individual cultures to develop in the region which differ from the southern norm.

It is not a mountainous country: the relief presents no barrier to its penetration as the Welsh hills do. The greater part of the land ranges from between 200 to 600 feet; only on Exmoor,

Fig. 1

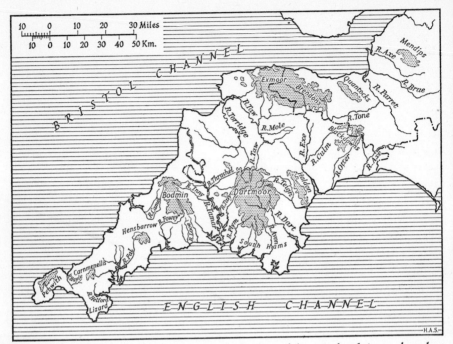

Fig. 1. Relief map of the South West, land over 1,000 feet is stippled; county boundaries are shown by a broken line

Dartmoor and Bodmin are there extensive areas above 1000 ft, and these are rolling grass and heather moorlands capable of supporting a considerable prehistoric population under favourable climatic conditions. Although on a small scale, the relief is readily distinguishable and forms the key to an understanding of the region. Early man, lacking maps, would soon have learnt to recognize the pattern of the hills and rivers. The 400–800 ft Land's End peninsula dominates the horizon of West Cornwall, as does Bodmin Moor, rising to 1375 ft, in East Cornwall. The mass of Dartmoor, with its summits of High Willhayes (2039 ft) in the north and Ryder's Hill (1692 ft) on the south is conspicuous on the skyline over the greater part of Devon, whilst the long west-to-east line of Exmoor (highest on Dunkery Beacon 1706 ft) with an extension in the Brendon

Hills (1340 ft) forms a landmark to the north. In the east the northern escarpment of the Blackdowns (800 ft) is also conspicuous, as well as the Quantock and Mendip ridges flanking the Somerset marsh. The principal rivers, the Exe, Teign, Dart, Plym, Tamar, Fowey and Fal, flow to the south coast: only the Taw and Torridge in mid-Devon, the Camel in Cornwall, and the Brue and Parrett in Somerset drain to the Bristol Channel. Consequently the south coast provides a succession of deep estuaries and natural harbours with a hinterland that is much dissected by steep-sided wooded valleys, whilst on the north there is an extensive coastal plateau, unbroken from the Camel to Hartland Point, lacking any sheltered anchorage.

In the main it is an ancient land, composed of Palaeozoic GEOLOGICAL and igneous rocks heavily worn down and eroded, with a suc- STRUCTURE cession of later formations overlying them in south-east Devon, and Somerset.

The earliest rocks make up the bold southerly promontories of the Lizard, Dodman and Bolt Head with Start Point. The remainder of the peninsula consists of the Devonian formations of sedimentary rocks, hard grits, sandstones, slates, limestones, and shales, which have been squeezed by north-south pressures into east-west folds in the Armorican earth movements at the close of the Carboniferous era. Exmoor and the Quantocks form the present summit of one such major fold; they dip southward into a great trough or syncline in mid-Devon in which the Carboniferous Culm Measures lie, and then rise again to reappear in south Devon and Cornwall. Pushed up into, and now appearing above them, are the five granite masses, Dartmoor, Bodmin Moor, Hensbarrow (St Austell), Carnmenellis, and Penwith, each surrounded by rocks altered by contact with the molten mass and known as the metamorphic aureole. Igneous rocks also intruded into the fissures that developed in the sedimentaries around the granite upheavals and gave rise to dykes, mainly of elvan, which show now as slender ridges or

17

bands of hard outcrop, some extending for several miles in Cornwall.

Overlying the eastern edge of the Culm are the New Red sandstones, the Permian and Triassic sands, marls and breccias, with a warm red colour which typifies the arid desert conditions at the time they were laid down. These extend from Torbay northwards and eastwards, and are conspicuous in the fields in the lower Exe and Culm valleys and in the eroded cliffs of the south coast as far as Sidmouth. Triassic marls also occur extensively in the Vale of Taunton. The succeeding Jurassic formations are marine deposits of Lias clay and limestones present in Somerset.

Finally, the Cretaceous formations are represented only in east Devon by a small coastal strip of chalk, best seen in the 300 ft cliff of Beer Head, with its seams of flint so important to early man, and by Greensand which forms a dissected plateau extending from the coast between Sidmouth and Lyme Regis and rising inland to form the Blackdown Hills. The Haldon ridge is a greensand outlier between the Exe and Teign valleys, which has a capping of chert and flinty gravel.

The low-lying area of the Somerset Levels is a trough eroded out of the soft Mesozoic sediments, which was filled after a marine transgression at the end of the glaciations by alluvial clays, and then by a succession of peats which were formed when the inland waters were ponded back by the estuarine muds and sand dunes of Bridgewater Bay. This peat growth continued, with fluctuations, during prehistoric and early historic times. The district thus became a fenland traversed by the narrow Lias ridge of the Polden Hills which divides the Brue and the Parrett.

SOILS

This outline of the geology indicates the variety of terrain that makes up the south-west and the different soils it contains. The Devonian sandstones produce a shallow, acid soil as on Exmoor, usually very stony, whilst the slates and killas in south

Devon and Cornwall break down into a 'shillet', that is, slivers of rock. The granite breaks up into a coarse gritty sand known as 'rab' in Cornwall or 'growan' in Devon. The patches of Devonian limestone in the hinterland of Torbay and at Plymouth produce a shallow calcareous soil. All these pervious soils over the Palaeozoic rocks have one thing in common, they nourish a woodland that is dry underfoot and free of undergrowth, which when it is cleared, produces good open grazing.

In contrast, the Culm Measures break down into a stiff yellow clay, water-logged in winter, hard-baked in summer, and supporting a dense mixed oakwood with a heavy undergrowth which rendered the greater part of mid-Devon unfit for early settlement. Nevertheless there are tracts where the bands of Culm sandstone or shale are exposed or near the surface, as in the Halwill district, north-west of Okehampton or in the Atlantic coastal tract between Stratton and Hartland; the soil here is lighter and better drained and consequently under favourable climatic conditions, as in the Bronze Age, these areas were occupied. The red soils of the Permian are deep, friable and fertile marls; they carry much woodland and therefore were not extensively settled till Saxon times. The Greensands produce acid sandy soils, often full of broken chert but suitable for early settlement.

The rainfall in the south-west, as is well known, is double   CLIMATE
that of south-east England; in Devon it averages today about 40 in. whilst on Dartmoor this rises to 80 in. or more in places. This is due to factors that are constant. The prevailing winds are westerly, warmed by their long passage across the Atlantic: rain-laden clouds impinge here first of all and discharge, or they descend in sea mists along the coasts or in hill-fogs on the moors. Great gales engendered in Biscay or far out on the Atlantic drive furiously across the peninsula, whipping up the seas and tearing at the trees. Consequently there are two contrary climatic factors affecting the western landscape: thus in

sheltered places well-watered vegetation grows lush in the warm and humid air, and even in winter the grass is green; but in exposed places, the trees are shorn and stunted by the winds and the moorlands have only a grass and heather covering which is bleak and austere. This in turn had consequences for early peoples in the region. Settlers looked for shelter from rain and wind for their huts, not in the deep valleys filled with luxuriant tree growth, but in those on the upland. Hill-forts were built not only on the crests, but on the hill-slopes, or tucked away down at the sheltered end of a spur, despite the loss of defensive advantage and outlook. Economically, the wet climate could be made an asset because it enabled herds of cattle to be built up to take advantage of the abundant grass and water supplies. On the other hand the uncertainties of large-scale corn-growing were avoided in a land where the stony ground was hard to till and the damp grain difficult to harvest and to store.

The varied geological structure provided early man with stones for building, for implements and ornaments and, above all, with metal ores.

Building stones confronted settlers practically everywhere; huts and enclosures were made of local material, particularly of the granite clitter on Bodmin, Dartmoor and Land's End. In so doing, people helped themselves by clearing the land of stones, improving the grazing or making some tillage possible. For the same reason most of the burial mounds in the region are cairns (that is, stone heaps) which were piled over a stone chamber or box-like cist.

This widespread use of stone is an advantage; stone structures survive, whilst wood and clay, the building materials of the rest of southern Britain, leave no surface trace. Since there has been little urban or industrial development in the region, a high proportion of monuments remain today in a setting that has not changed radically from prehistoric times. In districts like Dartmoor or West Penwith, groups of religious and funeral

Plate 45

Fig. 38

NATURAL
RESOURCES

Plate 46

Plates 20–22

20

monuments and numerous early settlements are preserved which give even the casual visitor a picture of early man in relation to his environment. For the archaeologist this wealth of material is a great asset; it is possible, for instance, to assess the number of households making up a community, to ascertain the acreage cultivated by a single family, or with the aid of excavation to ascertain their economy.

Fig. 27

On the other hand, the archaeologist is handicapped by the destructive character of the acid soils in most of the region. These dissolve human and animal bones, corrode bronzes to green powder and iron to shapeless lumps, and they soften the hand-made Bronze Age pottery, usually badly-fired and of poor clay in the first place, so that it disintegrates. Consequently finds from an excavation frequently are few and may give a mis-leading impression of poverty. Only in the bogs when the oxy-gen is excluded by the peat cover, or in the sands, do things survive well; at the Somerset lake villages of Meare and Glas-tonbury the decoration on wooden tubs is preserved and bronzes still retain their golden colour.

The real riches of the south-west are its mineral ores: of these, tin, copper, lead with its associated silver and some iron were utilised in prehistoric and Roman times. Metal-bearing lodes in Devon and Cornwall are intimately related to the gran-ite, since they are the products of vapours and solutions filling the fissures which developed as the molten rock mass cooled and solidified. Prolonged erosion through millennia exposed the surface of the veins and weathered them: swollen streams brought down pebbles of cassiterite from the tin lodes and de-posited them along with granite debris in the gravels of the river beds. In prehistoric times, the full potential of the region was never realised, since the lodes slope steeply downwards at $30°-45°$, and the greater part lies too deep to be reached until the development of modern mining machinery. Early man was dependent on finding outcrops that could be worked open-cast

METALS

Fig. 2

or by shallow adits, and in the case of tin, by digging in alluvial gravels. The veins of ore would attract attention in the first place by the reddening of the surrounding rock, as can still be seen in the cliffs at St Just. The dark tinstone (cassiterite) or the yellow glint of copper sulphide (calcopyrite) would also be conspicuous by the associated bands of white quartz, and their characteristic close texture and heavy weight would also have served as a guide.

The richness of the south-west in tin is well-known but it is less generally appreciated that copper, the other component of bronze, is also present, admittedly now at depth. Both minerals are found together in Cornwall, principally in the Land's

Fig. 2

End peninsula, in the Camborne-Redruth district, and south-east of Bodmin Moor. On Dartmoor stream tin is widely distributed in the river valleys and copper occurs in the metamorphic aureole, principally in the Dart valley above Buckfast and around Tavistock and Gunnislake. This distribution ensured that most of the best mining areas were accessible from the south coast, where as we have seen, there are good harbours and deep estuaries.

Silver and lead ores occur sporadically in Cornwall, in the Callington district as argentiferous copper, and at Combe Martin in north Devon; but until the introduction of a coinage at the end of the Iron Age, and the fashion for fine tableware in Roman times, silver was not in demand.

Iron ores too are present in the south-west and there is evidence that they were utilised in the later prehistoric period. Limonite could be recognised by its rusty colour or slaggy appearance and haematite by the red streak that a piece will give if rubbed on any flat surface, as well as by the weight. The lodes are associated with the granite, but being in the mineral group that crystallised at lower temperatures than tin or copper, they are found, for the most part, farther away. The deposits of specular haematite associated with the Dartmoor granite occur

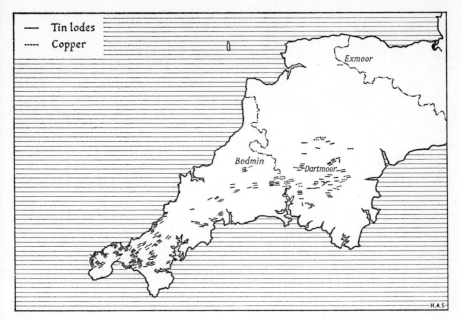

Fig. 2. Distribution of tin and copper lodes

in the lower Teign valley, and in Cornwall in the St Agnes
district. Iron oxides are also found in the overburden of the tin
and copper lodes forming the deposit known as gossan or 'iron
hat'. Small quantities of limonite occur as bog-iron concretions.

Mineral ores, then, are abundant, accessible and fairly widespread in the region. Man had to learn to recognise them as the
source of the different metals he successively required and to
discover different ways to transmute the stony ores into tactile
substances. The archaeological evidence for how this was a-
chieved is not straightforward. There is nothing comparable
with the late Bronze Age copper mines in the Austrian Tyrol,
for example, where the adits, tip-heaps and smelting places remain on the Schiefer Alp. In our region traces of shallow prehistoric or Roman workings have been obliterated by the systematic exploitation of historic times, and only scanty remains
of smelting hearths and small furnaces have occasionally been

Fig. 29

23

found in settlements. Fortunately there is the well-known account of tin working by the Greek historian Diodorus Siculus
(v: 22) writing in the 1st century B.C.; he narrates how the metal
was dug from earthy veins in the rock, ground down and
smelted into ingots shaped like knuckle-bones *(astragali)*, and
then carried across the sands in waggons to the island of St Michael's Mount *(Ictis)* at low tide. From here it was shipped by
Gallic traders to western ports in Gaul and then by an overland
route to the Mediterranean at the mouth of the Rhône. For the
rest, the periods at which the metal was worked have to be
inferred from the discovery of dateable objects in the mining
areas. Occasionally an exotic find from overseas or from other
parts of Britain reveals the source from which traders came to
buy. Irish merchants can thus be detected in Cornwall in the
early Bronze Age bringing gold lunulae, or Dobunnic merchants from the Cotswolds exchanging iron currency bars for
the local tin at Holne on the Dart. The south-west was not
Eldorado; it did not grow rich on its metals. Even in the Iron
Age when the tin trade was most flourishing, the Cornish
chieftains and their ladies had relatively few fine possessions and
for the mass of the people, the pastoral mode of life was little
changed. In Roman times, metals were a state monopoly and
therefore of little material benefit to the locality.

Plate 32

For traders and invaders coming to the south-west, seaways
were of more importance than landways. The southern flank
of the peninsula has a series of inviting entries by the dozen
rivers from the Axe to the Fal. Many of these are 'rias', drowned
river valleys formed when the sea levels rose in post-glacial
times. Their deep water channels could carry shallow-draught
vessels far inland, through the steep-sided lower reaches where
the green canopy of the woods in summer comes down to the
water, towards the moorland hills which beckoned on the horizon. Even today the Dart is navigable to Totnes, and before
the weirs were built, the tides ran up to Staverton, over 12

Fig. 1

miles from the coast. The estuaries also provide a sheltered anchorage from the westerly gales. Consequently, as the distribution of archaeological material will show, peoples coming from
western Europe aimed to make their landfall on this coast and
contacts with Dorset and southern England were fostered by
the ease of coastal traffic from Neolithic times onwards.

The stormy north Cornish coast has only St Ives Bay and
the Camel estuary at Padstow for voyagers approaching it from
the Irish sea or the Bristol Channel. From these ports it was
possible to cross the peninsula at its narrowest points, either to
the sandy expanse of Mounts Bay or, rounding the flank of
Bodmin Moor, to reach the navigable reaches of the Fowey: a
string of finds attest the use of these two trans-peninsular routes
in most periods.

Before the coming of the Roman engineer and the constructed
road with its straight alignment, travel was by ridgeway, by
unmetalled circuitous tracks which by sticking closely to the
watersheds avoid descents into the wooded valleys and the crossing of streams. The complicated structure of Devon and Cornwall, where the pattern of the relief is interrupted by the granite
masses, does not lend itself to a long-distance east-west route
comparable with the Icknield Way or the Berkshire ridgeway.
Instead there are a number of short north-south routes related
to the hill systems, such as those on the Greensand in east
Devon, or in the South Hams, or in the Looe-Fowey district
in south Cornwall. Their use is attested by the distribution of
barrows, hill-forts and chance finds.

On the rolling moorlands above the tree line there was greater
freedom of movement. The small streams on Bodmin and Dartmoor are not difficult to cross in the upper valleys, and the bogs
that are now obstacles have developed mainly since the climatic
deterioration early in the Iron Age, so traffic was not canalised.
In north Devon there is a ridgeway sign-posted by barrow
groups from the coast at Morte Bay to Blackmoor Gate, and

25

another going south-east on the high ground from Challacombe Common, on the line of the present county boundary.
In west Somerset the sparsely populated Brendon Hills are
linked with Exmoor and with the Blackdowns by an east-west
ridgeway and the Quantocks have a north-south route leading
to a crossing of the Tone at Taunton.

The difficulties of crossing the Somerset levels have already
been mentioned; in the late Bronze Age, when the climate rapidly deteriorated, timber tracks were laid on Shapwick Heath
for crossing the low ground to the Polden ridge along which
N.W.–S.E. traffic was always possible, 150 feet above the marshes. In sum, in the south-western peninsula, land-travel by
ridgeway or across open moor was possible for relatively short
distances in the areas suitable for occupation; long-distance
travel was by sea.

CHAPTER II

The Neolithic Peoples

IT IS ALWAYS DIFFICULT to decide at what point to launch into the stream of human history. The concern of the archaeologist in a region is with change and succession, with peoples' coming and going, with the development of tools and weapons, the variations in pottery-making, house or tomb building, and with the expansion or contraction of settlement areas: there are no fixed points at which to begin or end in the flow of time.

The arbitrary point selected in this book is the arrival in the south-west of a people from western France with a Neolithic culture, on present dating between 3300 and 3000 B.C. These were communities who had already mastered the arts of pottery making and of specialised flint working and who had knowledge of the raising and management of cattle and sheep, and of the cultivation of grain. The mixed economy of the west country farmer was theirs in embryo and they were tied to the soil, the seasons and their pastures as is their modern counterpart. In this they differed fundamentally from the earlier Mesolithic groups who were semi-nomadic, living by hunting, fishing and collecting of their food supplies.

At this time the country was much as we have described it in Chapter 1; with the exception of the high moorlands, a mixed oak forest had grown extensively in the warm wet Atlantic climate that had set in about 5000 B.C., succeeding the cold dry Boreal phase in which pine and birch forests predominated. Recent pollen analysis on Dartmoor by I. A. Simmons shows that the blanket peat bog began to form at this time and that oak and alder formed the highest proportion of the wind-borne tree pollens at its base, followed by wych-elm, birch and also a little lime. Similarly in the Somerset levels a marine transgression *circa* 4000 B.C. succeeded by freshwater swamps was a result of the same climatic amelioration; these were followed by the growth of alder and birch woods which in turn were swamped by the development of raised bogs with sphagnum before 2000 B.C.

The newcomers were experienced in forest clearance and had developed a characteristic tool, the stone axe, the endurance and efficiency of which was increased by polishing. With its aid, and by bark-ringing and burning, cultivation patches could be cut out of the forests, and the grazing of the livestock then kept the ground clear. A gradual amelioration of the climate in the second millenium B.C., the Sub-Boreal phase, also helped to check regeneration of the woods.

The people who formed the basis of the primary Neolithic population in the south-west are known as yet only from their settlements and from chance finds of their possessions. Their physical appearance, however, can be established from the skele-tons of their contemporaries inhumed under long barrows in southern England. They were of small stature, lightly boned and neatly built, with delicately fashioned hands and feet, in-dicating good powers of movement and skill; they had long thin faces, and probably a swarthy complexion, not unlike the the North American Indian. They arrived in southern England over a long period of time in the late fourth and third millennia B.C., bringing with them into the empty wooded lands their seed-corn, their stock and their skills in craft. The boats in which they travelled are not known but we may suppose it was in some sort of a skin-boat like the Irish curraghs which are seaworthy in the Atlantic swells.

In our area, the indigenous Mesolithic inhabitants were few and confined to the coasts and open moors. Their hearths and chipping floors at which microliths (tiny flint blades with blunt backs) were produced, have been found on the cliffs in Pen-with, on the north Cornish and Devon coasts and also around

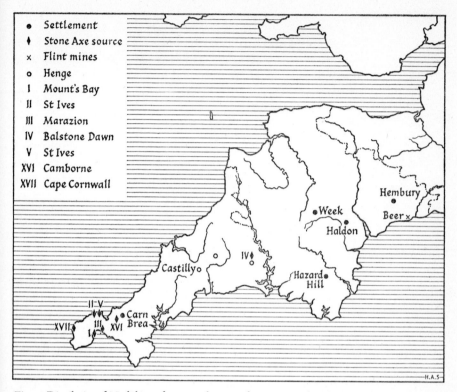

Legend:
- • Settlement
- ♦ Stone Axe source
- × Flint mines
- o Henge
- I Mount's Bay
- II St Ives
- III Marazion
- IV Balstone Dawn
- V St Ives
- XVI Camborne
- XVII Cape Cornwall

Fig. 3. Distribution of Neolithic settlements and centres of stone axe production

Dozemary Pool on Bodmin Moor. Little groups occur around spring heads, as at Week, Dartmoor, and on sand hills, as at Gwithian. They lived a precarious and semi-nomadic existence.

The distinctive group of Neolithic people who settled in south-west England were probably the earliest to arrive in southern Britain from the continent. Their settlements range from Carn Brea near Camborne to Maiden Castle in Dorset. The most important is the causewayed camp at Hembury, east Devon, which first produced the pottery that differentiates these south-western communities from the related Windmill Hill peoples of Wiltshire and Sussex, and which radiocarbon

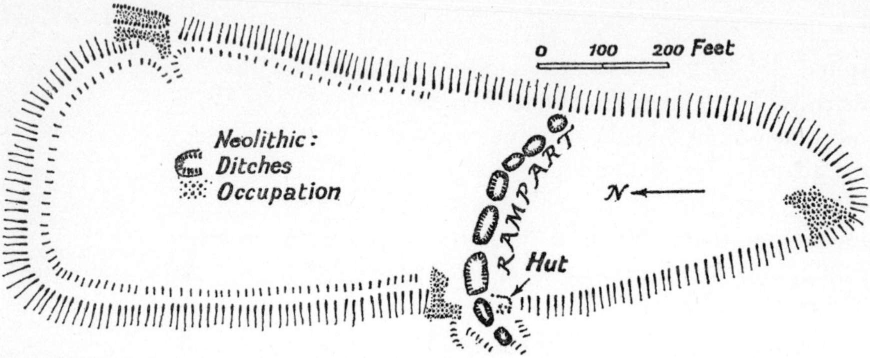

Fig. 4. Causewayed camp at Hembury, Devon. The hachures mark the inner rampart of the Iron Age hill-fort

analysis has now shown to have been occupied from about 3320–3000 B.C.

Hembury is on the tip of a steep-sided spur of greensand at the end of the Blackdown Hills, north-west of Honiton and about 12 miles from the coast. The site has obvious defensive advantages and consequently was strongly fortified by the Celtic people in the Iron Age, and it was during the systematic excavation of the hill-fort by the late Dorothy Liddell in 1930–35 that the Neolithic settlement came to light. The end of the spur was enclosed by eight lengths of ditches aligned as a segment of a circle across the ridge and the soil heaped up as a rampart on their south side. The ditches were of a characteristic U-shaped profile, and were separated by causeways of varying width which may have been left for no other reason than that sufficient soil had been obtained for the rampart. There was an entrance at the west end, where there was a setting of five posts in two rows across a causeway, a framework for some sort of gate or a barricade: immediately inside was a timber hut. The settlement, however, was not confined within the crescent of ditches and bank, but extended northwards to another ditch with an external palisade on the east side of the hill. Whether this was part of a second line of interrupted ditches crossing the

Plate 66

Fig. 4

spur could not be ascertained, owing to the overlying Iron Age defences, but it seems likely that Hembury consisted of two or more enclosures, like the majority of its kind. It thus represents the adaption of the concentric plan, familiar from Windmill Hill or the Trundle, to a promontory site. At Hambledon, Dorset, the outer zone of a Neolithic settlement was defined similarly by short lines of ditches across the spurs.

The Neolithic people lived in the lee of their ramparts and on the tip of the spur. Beneath the Iron Age deposits and covered by a band of sterile soil representing the vegetation that had grown over the hill after their settlement was abandoned, there was a thick layer of burning and occupation debris with stone-edged hearths and small shallow pits. Some of the pits had been used for food storage, as was shown by carbonised grain and hazel nuts: in one there was a complete bag-shaped pot so placed to keep liquid, such as curdled milk for cheese, safe from upset and at an even temperature. Other pits were probably ovens used for roasting meat or fish amongst heated stones and ashes. In time they ceased to be used and gradually filled up with rubbish, as is shown by Miss Liddell's discovery of a place 'where a pot of wheat had been upset, the grain lying thick upon the edge of the pit and spraying out over the slope'. With it was a large piece of pottery with grains adhering to its inner surface. The dwellings associated with all this activity were ill-defined, no more than a curved setting of stones and an occasional post-hole; they must have been lightly-built, with walls of wattle-work daubed over with clay on the stone base, and thatched with heather or reeds. Only the oval or sub-rectangular hut by the entrance – the so-called guard-house – had a substantial frame of 17 close-set posts. Occupation-rubbish was deposited in the ditches and burnt there; on top of the primary silt in most sectors there was a pronounced layer of burning in one place nearly 2 ft deep, which had reddened the ditch for 3 feet up the slope. Charcoal from this layer gave a

Plate 1

radiocarbon date of 3330 B.C. $\pm$ 150, which can be compared with 3240 B.C. $\pm$ 150 from charcoals from the occupation area, and 3300–3000 B.C. from a sample from the bottom of the ditch.

From the extent, density, and character of the occupation, Hembury appears to have been a permanent settlement for some 300–500 years. The frequency of grain in the pits, which a recent examination has shown to be emmer, a small wheat *(Triticum dioccum)* naked and hulled barley *(Hordeum)* and possibly also spelt *(Triticum spelta)* and of the saucer-shaped saddle querns for grinding, indicates that the occupants were arable farmers. The picture of their economy is necessarily incomplete because no animal bones survived in the acid soil; only the ubiquitous flint scrapers, of which 600 were found, attests to the preparation of skins for leather clothing, thongs, bags etc. and shows that they were also stock breeders.

Hembury, then, is a contrast with other causewayed camps in southern England where the occupation was sparse, limited to the neighbourhood of the ditches and apparently seasonal.

Fig. 3   A brief glance at the other hill-top settlements in the region shows that they are akin to Hembury. At Hazard Hill (400 ft) above the Harbourne river west of Totnes, a prolific flint industry was associated with pottery in small pits, hearths and cooking holes and with occasional post-holes dug in the shillet; saucer querns were also present, implying cultivation. The settlement was not enclosed. At Haldon, on the top of the

Fig. 5   800 ft ridge dividing the Exe and Teign and accessible by eight miles of ridgeway from the coast, the remains of a sizeable rectangular house was found. It had a frame of timber uprights 2 to 4 feet apart and a gabled roof carried on a ridge-pole indicated by two post-holes on the central axis. The daub walls rested on a rough foundation of small stones set in clay, with a doorway in the north-east corner and there was a stone-edged hearth in the south-east angle. The clay floor was trodden hard

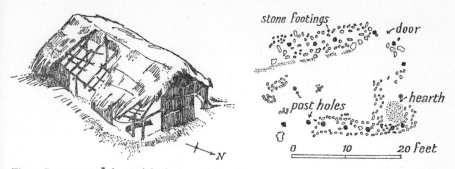

Fig. 5. Reconstruction of a Neolithic house at Haldon, Devon

and had been raised and renewed: a thick deposit of ash against the north wall and partly underlying it, also indicated a long occupation. Like Hazard, the settlement was apparently open; the impression of a grain of wheat on a potsherd indicates that corn was grown here also.

At Carn Brea near Redruth, Cornwall, the settlement was on the south-east flank of the 700 ft hill, which was fortified later by the Iron Age people. Characteristic western Neolithic pottery was found here below the floors of huts belonging to the hill-fort when these were excavated in the nineteenth century, as well as several stone axes and many leaf-shaped flint arrowheads.

The domestic pottery produced by these people is nearly all plain ware, wide-mouthed bowls and baggy pots with unsteady rounded bases and simple flat or pinched-out rims: many have lugs to lift them with, either solid little bosses or perforated vertically for a thong. These basic shapes are common to a wide range of early Neolithic peoples both in Britain and in western Europe, as at the first lake settlement at Cortaillod, Switzerland. Of special importance because they are peculiar to the south-west are bowls with big incurved lugs, perforated horizontally and christened 'trumpet lugs' from their expanded ends: analogies for these are found in the earlier wares from the Camp de Chassey in the Massif Central and in a few megalithic tombs in Brittany, Castellic and Kervilor. A few

POTTERY

Plate 1

Plate 2

bowls from Hembury and some others coming principally from Carn Brea have a carination break below a straight neck, a specialised western form that differs from the hollow-necked variety at Windmill Hill, and which appears in settlements at Clegyr Boia, Pembrokeshire and at Lough Gur in Co. Cork and are probably of later date.

Though the shapes are unsophisticated, the fabric is surprisingly good, better than much Bronze Age pottery. Most of it is a coarsely gritted black or brownish ware, sometimes with a smooth leathery finish. There is also a thin red ware in which the fine grits are of a tremolite schist derived from the metamorphic rocks, probably from the eastern flank of Dartmoor. The bowls with trumpet lugs at Hembury are of this ware (the f. ware), which has also been recognised at Haldon, Hazard Hill and Gwithian in west Cornwall. Recent analysis by Mr H. Hodges shows that similar grits of igneous origin occur in the pottery from the causewayed camps at Maiden Castle, Windmill Hill, and Robin Hood's Ball, Wiltshire. It seems that there was a long-distance as well as a local movement in this better-class ware from the south-west.

Plate 2

A flat-based pot from Haldon decorated with two zones of incised vertical lines stands rather apart from this series, although it was associated with it on the site. It may be a later product of the group comparable with Rinyo-Clacton decorated wares in the south and east.

Plate 10

FLINT-WORKING

The stone industry of these early Neolithic peoples indicates even more clearly than the pottery, their capacity to exploit the local resources and to organise long-distance travel. In Cornwall beach flint was used but in Devon the material for the numerous leaf-shaped arrowheads, scrapers and blades was the mottled blue or black unpatinated flint from the chalk at Beer Head. The mining places at Beer have not been located but there are many hollows and waste heaps just below the edge of the 400 ft plateau, at a level which coincides with the bands of

Fig. 3

flint nodules exposed in the cliffs. Flint-working floors are fre-quent on the chalk plateau of the Head, an area of about 2½ square miles; only small implements were made here, rough-outs for axes being significantly absent. The amount of flint waste at Hembury, Haldon and Hazard Hill, shows that it was the raw material that was sought at Beer, not finished prod-ucts. The communities must have made regular visits by ridge-way or by sea, landing in the shelter east of Beer Head. Some flint axes were apparently imported ready-made from the chalk farther east: fifteen were found at Hembury of a grey patinated flint and about twenty more have been recorded as surface finds from Cornwall and Devon. The distribution indicates sea trade, with entries at Mounts Bay and Plymouth Sound.

This trade in axes was a two-way trade: the Neolithic peoples of the chalk were ready to purchase polished axes of the sombre igneous rocks, the greenstones of the south-west, which had blades less liable to fracture and were so different in appearance from the flint in general use. The sources of stone axe produc-tion are now known from petrological analysis, undertaken from 1937 onwards by Dr F. S. Wallis and the late Dr J. F. S. Stone for a committee of the South West Museums. By cutting a thin section from an axe and examining it microscopically it is pos-sible to identify the constituents of the rock and to study their form and arrangement; on this basis a high proportion of the axes have been classified into 19 groups and closely related sub-groups. It has been possible to match exactly some of these sections with specimens of actual rocks and thus identify, with-in close limits, their places of manufacture both in Cornwall and elsewhere. This cannot always be done because the com-position of the metamorphic rocks is highly variable and may change even in one exposure, and the variation may not be recorded in the available geological collections. However, greenstone axes of Groups II and V have been shown to ema-nate from St Ives, Group III from Trenow, Marazion, Group

THE AXE
TRADE

Fig. 3

IV from Balstone Down, Callington, and Group XVI from near Camborne, and XVII from Kenidjack Castle, in Penwith: in the case of the prolific Group I, the Mousehole-Penzance district is indicated but the actual outcrop is probably now submerged. Groups IA, IIA, IIIA, IVA, and XIX remain unmatched, although Cornwall is probably their most likely source.

Despite these indications from the petrologists, archaeologists have not yet discovered any of the Cornish quarries or factories. Elsewhere, at Graig Lwyd in Caernarvonshire and Great Langdale in Cumberland for instance, the sites have been located from the heaps of waste and incomplete or broken tools. It is evident from the number of south-western axes that cannot be grouped that small outcrops were used from time to time; such as an axe from Natton Hole, Drewsteignton, from a neighbouring outcrop of hornfels, and one from Otterton, east Devon, made of a greenstone localised at Lay Point, St Ives, the sole example of Group III.

Fig. 6

The extent to which these axes travelled is well shown by the distribution of Group I; the concentration in Penwith indicates that local needs were first supplied; a few went to communities in mid-Cornwall and south Devon, where one was found at Hazard Hill, but most of the output went to Wessex, from which over 60 axes have been identified. The route evidently was by sea to Dorset, and thence by the Avon to Salisbury Plain, and across Pewsey Vale to the Marlborough Downs. Others went by the Bristol Channel to the Mendips and Cotswolds. Finds in Sussex, the lower Thames valley and Essex also indicate long-distance coastal traffic: clearly some of these western Neolithic peoples maintained their practice of seagoing long after the immigration. In this connection the discovery of an unusual type of greenstone adze with a quantity of decayed wood thought to be a boat in the Red River gravels at Tuckingmill, Camborne, is significant.

Fig. 6. Distribution of Cornish stone axes, Group I type

We can distinguish five early factories, IIA, IV, IVA, XVI and XVII producing axes exclusively. The early Neolithic date for factory IVA was established at Maiden Castle where six specimens were recovered from the occupation of the primary causewayed camp, which was abandoned and built over by a long Bank barrow in late Neolithic times. Other axes from this and the other factories have been found at Hembury and Hazard, both early sites. Most of the exports did not go beyond Somerset, Devon or Dorset but it appears from an axe of Group IIA found at Windmill Hill that some Cornish trade with the central Wessex area was in existence by 2500 B.C. The trade must have built up gradually as the population grew, as the

coasts became known and the hazards of the long journey overcome. Since some of the Windmill Hill pottery is made of the
western clays, the merchant-venturers probably included some
fine wares in their cargo containing their own seasonal food
supplies and suitable for barter or gifts.

The later factories are I, IA, III and IIIA, which produced
mainly axes but also axe-hammers, battle-axes, maces and
pounders, predominantly for the Wessex market. Several specimens have been found in late Neolithic and Beaker contexts
in Wiltshire as at Woodhenge and West Kennet avenue, showing that production continued during the period 2000–1600
B.C. The production of the new shaft-holed implements characteristic of the latter part of this epoch shows that the Cornish
producers were susceptible to the demands of the new Beaker
and Wessex chiefs.

Organised traffic routes on land are in evidence in the Somerset levels where three timber trackways dated by radiocarbon
analysis to the third millenium B.C. have been discovered in
peat cutting. The tracks were made on the drying surface of
the reed fen and also on the humified peat of the raised bogs
which superseded it: they cross the low-lying ground between
the River Brue and the Polden ridge near Shapwick. The tracks
were narrow, 2–5 feet wide, and constructed of hazel rods and
thin birch timbers and covered with brushwood laid across
them: in one instance the track was held in position in the
yielding peat by obliquely driven stakes. Radiocarbon dates
from the wood in the three tracks at Shapwick – Honeygore,
Blakeway and Honeycat – show that these date from within
130 years of 2800, 2500, and 2200 B.C. respectively.

LATE
NEOLITHIC
SETTLEMENT
Evidence for late Neolithic settlements in the region is at
present derived from surface observations. On the chalk where
flint is native to the soil a scatter of flakes and broken implements is not remarkable, but in the west where flint is 'imported' it is significant if dateable artifacts are associated with

surface waste. A systematic study of an area near Week on the north-eastern foothills of Dartmoor has demonstrated the existence of 16 small settlements, occupied intermittently over a long period of time. The sites are by the springheads and extend over a mile and a half of south-facing slopes. The flint waste is concentrated round the spring in patches covering from half to two acres and gradually thinning out. The artifacts collected after ploughing number over 30,000 and were associated with quantities of burnt stones, indicative of cooking and pot-boiling. The sites were first occupied intermittently by Mesolithic hunting groups: they produced pygmy tools, obliquely-blunted, triangular and hollow-based points, blades and gravers and the abundant waste products characteristic of a microlithic industry. Occupation in Neolithic times is indicated by five green-stone axes, one from the Balstone Down factory (Group IV), and by over 50 leaf-shaped and 40 transverse (*petit-tranchet* and derivatives) arrowheads. There is also a shale amulet and a mace-hammer, both with an hour-glass perforation made by pecking on both sides of the stone before the art of through drilling with abrasive was mastered. Ripple-flaked plano-convex knives and a few barbed and tanged arrowheads show that the occupation continued into the early Bronze Age. Similar discoveries of surface flints as at Mutters Moor, near Sidmouth or Orleigh near Barnstaple or in the Torbay district show that this open settlement pattern was not uncommon.

We can recognise in such communities the Secondary Neolithic people of the south-west, possessing a stone equipment owing something to both old and new ideas. The flint work with its high proportion of *petit-tranchet* arrowheads and their derivatives reveal a Mesolithic element in the population, but the axes and leaf arrowheads are types normal to the primary Neolithic agriculturalists. Without excavation it is impossible to say whether they possessed any pottery that differs from the Hembury-Haldon range. In southern and eastern Britain highly decorated wares were produced by groups with a similar mixed flint industry, both the corded, stamped and pitted Ebbsfleet and Peterborough bowls or the grooved and incised Rinyo-Clacton flat-based pots. Isolated specimens of Peterborough ware have been found in Somerset, at Rowbarrow cave on Mendip and at the base of the peat on Meare Heath, dating about 2300 B.C., but none farther west.

HENGES

It is likely that some religious monuments were built by the late Neolithic peoples: these are the henge monuments with a single entrance (Atkinson's Class I), at which grooved and rusticated Rinyo-Clacton pottery has been found in southern Britain and for which a radiocarbon date of 2400–2100 B.C. has been obtained at Arminghall, Norfolk. Those recognised are Castilly and Castlewich in east Cornwall and less certainly in the Roseland peninsula on the Fal and on Parracombe Common, Exmoor. The best preserved is Castilly on Innis Down near Lanivet, which has an oval arena 97 by 161 feet surrounded by a barrier ditch with a broad external bank and an entrance opening north-west; the monument seems designed for ceremonies to be viewed by spectators on the bank. Excavations in 1962 did not produce any dateable finds.

Fig. 3

Plate 4

It is not known whether these western henges had a setting of stones or timber posts like most of their southern counterparts, or what is their relationship to the free-standing stone circles on the moors. The Stripple Stones circle on Bodmin Moor has a low surrounding bank dug from an external ditch which suggests there was some continuity between the two types of monument and that it remained important to prevent trespass on a sacred enclosure.

To sum up this first phase of colonisation, we have an intrusive people, primarily agriculturalists coming in discrete parties from north-western France, and entering by the southern coasts to settle in the adjacent lowland. They exploited the various metamorphic rocks for material for the stone axes they needed in clearing the woodland and built up gradually a flourishing trade with their contemporaries in southern Britain. In the course of time some mixing with the indigenous Meso-lithic stock took place, giving rise to communities with slightly different flint tools and arrows. The distribution shows that the communities were few and, apart from the Land's End peninsula, the land was sparsely settled.

CHAPTER III

The Megalithic Peoples

SO FAR AS IS KNOWN at present, no burial places can be specifically connected with the early Neolithic peoples in Devon or Cornwall. The impetus to build the great stone tombs to be described in this chapter appears to have come from new arrivals with a similar stone economy and way of life. We cannot, however, be certain of this because the majority of tombs have been ransacked and very little pottery or other grave-goods have been recovered to compare with anything found in the causewayed camps and other settlements.

The new tombs were family vaults, spaciously and elaborately constructed for successive burials. The funeral rites included the lighting of fires and the digging of small pits to receive libations, funeral feasts and animal sacrifices, and a ceremonial blocking of the entrance to the tomb after each interment. The labours, skill, and care devoted by a primitive people to the construction of these tombs shows the importance that the ancestral dead had attained in their thoughts: we may reasonably suppose they were compelled to do so by a religious cult or belief.

The development of tomb-building in the south-west is a phenomenon common to the western seaboards of Britain and Ireland in Middle and Late Neolithic times. It originated in movements of peoples from Spain, Portugal, and southern France up the Atlantic coasts to Brittany and eventually into the Irish sea. Broadly speaking, the megalithic peoples can be divided into builders of Gallery Graves – elongated rectangular tombs as the name implies, entered directly, and usually covered by a long mound – and builders of Passage Graves, in which the tomb chamber is usually sub-circular and approached by a passage leading in from the edge of a round mound or cairn.

It is generally held that the initial movement to Britain was by builders of Gallery Graves into South Wales and Gloucestershire (the SevernCotswold group) and up the Irish Sea to southwest Scotland and Northern Ireland (the ClydeCarlingford group) to be followed later by Passage Grave builders to eastern and southern Ireland (the Boyne group) and from these, expansion and a secondary colonisation of the coastlands bordering the Irish sea took place during the second half of the third millennium. In the process, the tomb architecture was modified and both elaborate and degenerate forms were evolved, so that in some late examples, it is hard to perceive their origin or affinities.

In the southwest four classes of tombs can be distinguished, all built of large stones, mainly granite, from which the modern generic name, *megalith*, is derived, which has replaced the former Celtic *cromlech* or *dolmen*. They are (i) Gallery Graves with simple rectangular tombchambers, terminally situated in long mounds or cains; (ii) Penwith tombs, similar squarish chambers covered by a round cairn; (iii) one example of a Passage Grave; and (iv) Entrance Graves, which are gallerylike chambers placed at the edge of a round mound, and are derivatives of Passage Graves.

The distribution is coastal with a concentration in the case of classes ii and iv in the Land's End peninsula. Entry of immigrants by the Camel estuary on the north coast is indicated by some of the Gallery Graves, whilst others landing on the south coast penetrated to the edge of Dartmoor, but not into east Devon. Most of the tombs are inconspicuously sited, on hillsides and the edges of plateau country, and in the case of the Entrance Graves at Pennance and Brane even in a little valley. It may be surmised that these places were chosen because they were close to the settlements. Some, however, are crestsited; the long mound of Corringdon Ball, South Brent, is on a saddle at 1100 ft between the Avon and its tributary, the

Fig. 7

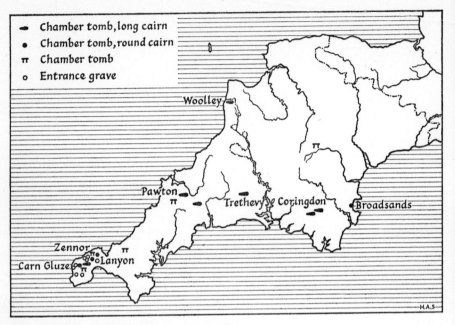

Fig. 7. Distribution of chamber tombs and Entrance Graves

Glaze brook, and though concealed when approached along the ridge, is dominant on the skyline when seen from the west across the brook. Such sites probably were chosen because they were conspicuous in the view of the living.

GALLERY
GRAVES

Fig. 8

These tombs are characterised by a long or oval mound, of which the best preserved are at Pawton, Corringdon Ball and Woolley, standing 4, 6 and 12 feet high respectively. At Lani‑vet, Trethevy and Lanyon, the cairns are only just discernible because material has been removed by farmers for wall building, whilst Spinsters' Rock, Dresteignton and Pendarves Park, Camborne, have been wholly denuded. Normally the mound or cairn was built up to the level of the chamber and functioned as a ramp up which the heavy capstones were dragged on rol‑lers, and as a platform from which they could be manoeuvred

44

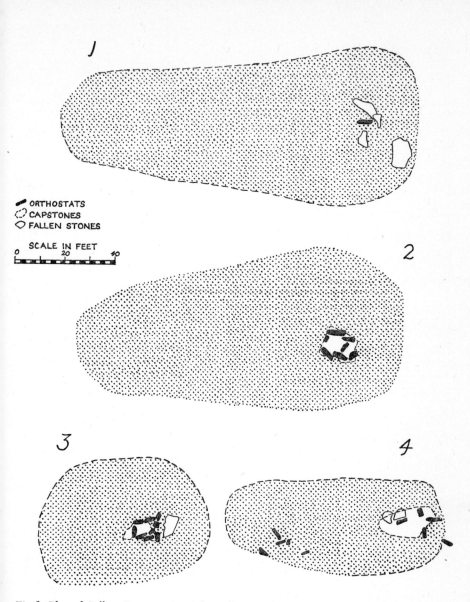

Fig. 8. Plans of Gallery Graves. 1. Corringdon Ball; 2. Trethevy; 3. Pawton; 4. Lanyon

Within the figure:

_1_

ORTHOSTATS
CAPSTONES
FALLEN STONES

SCALE IN FEET
0   20   40

_2_

_3_

_4_

into position. Lacking modern excavation, it is not known whether the cairns were built with internal revetment walls or marginal slabs (peristalith), or whether any of them were constructed with a fore-court to the chamber, as is usual in Gallery Graves.

The tomb chambers have also suffered by the removal of stones: at Lanivet, Bodmin, only the great capstone measuring 10 ft by 16 ft and two supporters remain, whilst at Corringdon Ball what was left of the chamber has collapsed in a tumble of slabs. Lanyon, Pendarves and Spinsters' Rock also collapsed in recent times and what we now see are nineteenth century reconstructions. The tomb at Pawton, near Wadebridge is better preserved and would repay scientific excavation. The closed chamber, half-full of soil, is towards the broad end of the 70 ft oval mound. It is covered by a thick capstone 10 ft long by 7 ft wide, now bearing on three of the seven uprights that constitute the chamber; formerly the capstone was 3 ft longer, a piece having cracked off and fallen forwards; when unbroken it would have rested on two other half-buried uprights which, with the front supporter, formed in effect, a shallow façade in front of the closed chamber. This is an important feature because it links this Cornish megalith with others in the south, in which the deep stone-lined forecourt characteristic of the Gallery Graves of the Clyde-Carlingford group has been reduced to a façade. Pawton is thus connected with Pentre Ifan in Pembrokeshire and with the Grey Mare and her Colts in West Dorset, both tombs with a shallow crescentic façade in front of a closed chamber.

Trethevy, St Clear, south of Bodmin Moor also has a closed chamber, but with side stones that project forwards to form an antechamber. The entrance to the inner tomb was by a small aperture in the bottom corner of the enormous granite slab that divides it from the antechamber, through which it is just possible to crawl. A restricted entry to megalithic tombs is quite

Plate 3

Fig. 8

Plate 6

common, reflecting the natural desire of a primitive people to keep the spirits of the dead in the tomb, despite the difficulties of inserting fresh bodies for burial when the occasion arose. Devices vary for narrowing the entry; some, like Trethevy, utilise natural cleavage or introduce small blocking stones, but in some tombs, not confined to any one class, a round hole was laboriously pecked out of a slab. Two of these so-called 'portholes' are found in Cornwall, though neither tomb has survived: the Maen-an-Tol, Madron and the Tolvaen at Gweek, both worked in the granite.

There is no evidence from grave-goods for the date or cultural affinities of the south-western Gallery Graves. The only indication that they were built for inhumations, and therefore of early origin, comes from West Lanyon, a tomb now practically destroyed but found intact about 1800. The 13 ft capstone had apparently slipped during construction and then had been covered by the mound. Digging in the chamber produced half a skull, thigh bones and other human bones, 'lying in a promiscuous state and a disordered manner', and above them 'a broken urn with ashes', presumably a Bronze Age cremation succeeding the primary collective burials. For although W.C. Borlase held that the bones belonged to a single inhumation, it is now recognised that disarticulate and disordered bones are characteristic of successive or collective interments, being the remains of earlier burials that have been pushed aside or rearranged to make room for a later one.

The Penwith tombs are smaller monuments: the remains of their circular cairns range from 32 to 40 ft in diameter and the closed chambers, though covered by large capstones, are not much bigger than large cists. They are all conspicuously sited above the 400 ft contour on the little hills of the Land's End peninsula.

Of the four or five examples, Zennor Quoit is the most interesting structurally and archaeologically, though the monument

PENWITH
TOMBS

Fig. 7

Plate 5

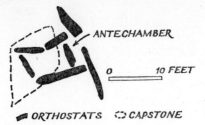

Fig. 9. Plan of the tomb chamber of Zennor Quoit, west Cornwall

Fig. 9

Fig. 10

Fig. 11

now differs from its original form. In the eighteenth century when William Borlase drew it, the 18 ft capstone was horizontal; its present tilt is due to the removal of supporters to make a nearby cart-shed. Like Trethevy, Zennor has an antechamber formed by projecting side-supporters and by two fine slabs set up with their outer faces at right angles to the long axis of the chamber, again a sort of façade confronting those who approached. There is a small space between the uprights to enter the antechamber but the main chamber is closed. Some casual digging in the main chamber by R. J. Noall produced some cremated bones, five flint flakes and the remains of a small biconical pot and the rim of another decorated with diagonal grooving. Previously, in 1881, a farmer named Grenfell and his son had delved under the paving in the antechamber, breaking up two slabs by blasting and finding underneath a perforated whetstone of a type found in early Bronze Age graves in

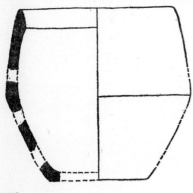

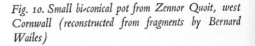

Fig. 10. Small bi-conical pot from Zennor Quoit, west Cornwall (reconstructed from fragments by Bernard Wailes)

Fig. 11. Whetstone from Zennor Quoit, west Cornwall. Original 3¼ in. high

Wessex. Part of a third pot with cord ornament also probably came to light on this occasion. Both groups of finds can now be recognised as of Bronze Age date: the grooved ware has anal[,] ogies in domestic pottery from Gwithian (layer 5) and from Dartmoor, and the biconical pot with others in Scilly. If the pos[,] ition of the whetstone be accepted, it appears that Zennor Quoit was not built till about 1600–1500 B.C. This need not surprise us for whilst the antechamber with its façade link it with the Gallery Graves, the round mound which survives at other Penwith tombs indicates contact with the Passage Graves and their late derivatives, the Entrance Graves.

There is only one tomb in the south-west that has claims to be recognised as a Passage Grave, the wrecked chamber and denuded cairn at Broadsands, Paignton. It is sited on the south-facing slopes above a sandy inlet on Torbay and within easy reach of a tract of open limestone country. Excavations by C. A. R. Radford showed that the chamber was polygonal, built of eleven small orthostats, 3–5 ft high, with the interstices

PASSAGE
GRAVES
Fig. 12

49

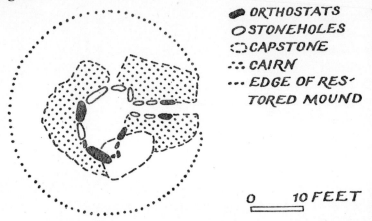

ORTHOSTATS
○ **STONEHOLES**
▭ **CAPSTONE**
∴ **CAIRN**
... **EDGE OF RES-
TORED MOUND**

O   10 FEET

Fig. 12. Plan of the Broadsands Passage Grave, Devon

filled with dry-stone walling, and roofed by a single slab. It was entered by a very narrow passage, built of small stones through-out; the cairn was probably circular, and 40 ft in diameter. The tomb has apparently been used over a period of time: the latest burial was a flexed inhumation of a young adult male with which was associated a collared rim sherd of decorated late Neolithic pottery; of the earlier burials only a few bones be-longing to two adult males and an infant were found trodden into the floor of the chamber. With these were fragments of western Neolithic pottery, including some from carinated bowls like those from Carn Brea. It was apparent that the first burials in the tomb had been cleared away, purifying fires had then been lit and the chamber roughly paved, before the last body had been placed in the tomb.

The indications are that this tomb with its two periods of inhumations is of early date, despite its small size and poor con-struction. Radford indeed has claimed that it is directly related to the classic Pavia type of Iberian tomb, such as Alcarapinha I, Alentejo, in central Portugal. Analogies with some Passage Graves in north-western France, with Parc Guren I in the

Morbihan, with Pleneuf in the Côtes du Nord and with La Sergenté in Jersey have also been suggested, though these are all much more imposing structures, the products of well-established communities. The builders of Broadsands can only be regarded as some bold voyagers who out-distanced their contemporaries and were alone in gaining a foothold on the southern coast.

The other group of people who have claims to be of Passage Grave descent are the builders of the Entrance Graves in Penwith. The tombs are all very similar: there is no passage and the narrow rectangular chamber with a ceiling of flat slabs, like a stone cupboard, is entered directly at the edge of a small conical mound, 15–25 ft in diameter, 6–10 ft high, which has a conspicuous kerb of large boulders. Good examples can be seen at Treen, Pennance and Brane in the Land's End peninsula. Many others are found in the Scilly Isles, the granite archipelago situated 28 miles out in the Atlantic, and there can be little doubt that it was from here that the colonists came to the mainland. At this time the Scillies were one island with a coast line approximating to the present 10 fathom line and consequently there was more cultivable flat land available to support the population. A few other tombs of this kind are found in south-east Ireland, round Tramore, representing another line of maritime expansion.

In the Scillies there is evidence of the formal development of these tombs and of their use and date. In the earliest examples on St Mary's, an upright slab marks the division between the passage and the chamber, and in another, Bants Cairn, the entry to the chamber is shown by projecting slabs in the side walls of the passage, which are the ends of an interior encircling revetment wall. In the later examples, the division between passage and tomb has disappeared and we are left with the Entrance Grave, which confusingly looks like a covered gallery and was so referred to by Hencken.

ENTRANCE GRAVES

Plate 11

51

The tombs initially were built to contain inhumations, for 'skeletal debris' was found in the floor of Obadiah's barrow on Gugh in 1900 but most held inurned cremations placed successively in the tomb. At Knackyboy on St Martin's, no less than 22 urns were recovered from about half of one of these graves, the other half having been previously rifled. The first interments in decorated biconical urns were set in hollows on the roughly paved floor and ashes from the pyre heaped over them; later, straight-sided urns were placed on top of them so that the low vault was filled nearly to the roof with tiers of crushed and broken pots. In the ashes associated with the first cremations were eight blue glass beads and one star-shaped bead of faience, an imported type that can be dated to the Middle Bronze Age, *c.* 1300 B.C. The forms of both types of urns are Bronze Age and there can be little doubt that Scillonian Entrance Graves were being used until a late date, perhaps even after 1000 B.C. Nevertheless they are collective tombs, very different from the single graves normal to the Bronze Age and in this sense their builders must be regarded as a megalithic people, even though they were using bronze for their tools and weapons; isolated in the islands, they were conservative of the old rites and beliefs concerning the dead.

None of the urn burials from the mainland have survived – the cupboards are bare – but here too the form of tomb persisted to a late date with the cairn enlarged and conspicuously sited on hilltops in the customary Bronze Age manner. At Tregaseal, St Just, a perforated whetstone similar to that from Zennor Quoit was found with cremated bones and pottery, since lost, on the floor of the tomb in the centre of a large oval cairn: a secondary cremation was in an adjoining cist, placed in a large ribbon-handled urn (p. 77): both burials should date from the early Middle Bronze Age, *c.* 1500–1300 B.C. At Carn Gluze, a great walled cairn on the cliffs at St Just, a typical Entrance Grave in the outer perimeter clearly was later than the corbelled

Plate 9

Plate 39

Fig. 11

Plate 36

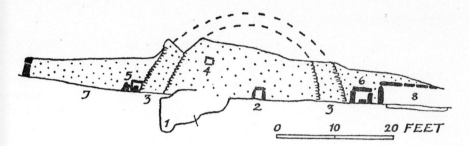

Fig. 13. Reconstructed section of Carn Gluze, St Just, west Cornwall (after W. C. Lukis). 1. primary pit; 2. four cists; 3. domed cairn; 4–6. Cists; 7. cairn ring; 8. Entrance Grave

structure in the centre of the cairn which contained at least one small pot of Middle or Late Bronze Age type.

Carn Gluze is a very remarkable structure: it was excavated in 1874 by W. C. Borlase and a gang of local miners, and although many details of construction have been lost, the plans made by W. C. Lukis are informative. In the light of recent knowledge, the following sequence can be deduced. The primary construction was a T-shaped pit (1), which was excavated 7 ft deep in the rocky subsoil and entered by rough steps cut in its sloping shaft; it contained only greasy mould in which a stone bead or amulet was found. The pit may have held an inhumation burial, the bones having dissolved in the acid soil, or more likely, it was a sacred pit, a symbolic entry to the underworld. Round the top of the pit-shaft there were four small cists (2) surrounded by remains of burning and containing miniature pots, one a bucket-shaped urn of late Middle Bronze Age form. These probably held offerings of food or drink, since only two minute pieces of bone were found in them. The second construction was an oval double-walled cairn (3) 30 ft by 37 ft with a domed surface and still surviving to a height of 12 ft. Its two walls, which are 5 ft apart and which pass over the primary pit, were corbelled inwards and the space between loosely filled with pitched slabs. At the same time, the little cists were covered with stones, which helped to support the

Plates 7, 8

Fig. 13

corbelled revetment walls of the rising dome. When this packing was 5 ft deep, another cist (4) was built containing pottery and the bones of a lamb, probably a final offering to the spirits of the underworld. There was no entry to the dome; but at the base of the outer wall, Borlase found a spread of charcoal and two more empty cists (5–6), one covered by tilted slabs. Finally the dome itself was encased by a massive cairn-ring (7) 18–20 ft wide, 4–5 ft high and walled externally. The Entrance Grave (8) was built in the south-west segment of the cairn-ring, more or less on the same axis as the shaft to the original pit, and in a line with one of the external cists. It alone was in contact with the outside world; quantities of burnt human bones and broken potsherds were found beneath its paved floor, though the last interments in the chamber had disappeared. Its marginal position is significant; at Carn Gluze this tomb is external to a concealed sacred place, in which an underworld cult had been practised in all probability.

Plate 8

Something similar can be seen in a Bronze Age turf barrow at Sixwells, Glamorgan but on a much smaller scale; this had a ritual pit in the centre, a hole only 9 inches in diameter, an enclosure marked by a circle of stakes and a cremation in a cist on its margin. The double-walled dome at Carn Gluze, however, has a megalithic ancestry: analogous dry-stone structures can be seen in the long cairns of some Severn-Cotswold Gallery Graves, namely the drum-like 'rotunda' covering a cist in the centre of the cairn at Notgrove, and the double-walled structure at Ty-Isaf, Breconshire, which surrounded the principal transepted-chamber at the tail-end of the cairn.

CHAPTER IV

The Beaker and Food-Vessel Peoples

T HE BEGINNING of the second millennium B.C. saw another element added to the already mixed Neolithic population in the south-west; a small group of the dynamic Beaker folk, whose advent paved the way for the development of Bronze Age society in this region as elsewhere in Britain. They were of continental origin, originally from Spain but spreading rapidly north and east, on the one hand by sea to north-west France and on the other overland to central Europe, Germany and the Netherlands. They were physically distinct from the Neolithic stocks, a race of powerfully built, short, ugly men and women, with round heads and prominent brow-ridges. They differed fundamentally from their predecessors in their burial rite, which was individual interment, usually under a small round cairn, instead of in a communal tomb. The assertion of the individual in this way in place of the ancestral family group implies a major re-orientation in society. Their basic possessions were those of the bowman, a figure skilled both as warrior and hunter like the dreaded North American Indian. Their wooden bows and quivers have perished but their barbed flint arrowheads, and hunters' knives of copper or of flint survive in the graves. Such equipment implies a different way of life from that of the settled Neolithic cultivators; it explains their great mobility and the rapidity with which they established their ascendancy. In central Europe, they participated in the winning and working of copper and there is little doubt that they were instrumental in spreading the knowledge and techniques of the new metallurgy.

Their name, as is well known, is derived from their characteristic pottery vessel, the beaker, made of highly ornamented thin red ware, which owes its colour and texture to skilled firing at a high temperature, probably in some form of kiln, with a forced draught, a technique acquired for smelting. From variations in the shapes, and to a lesser extent the decoration of the pottery, together with the associated grave-goods, it has been possible to identify several intrusive groups in Britain, and their continental sources. The first people who crossed the North Sea from the Rhine and the Netherlands to land on the eastern and southern coasts of England were makers of what is termed the B group of beakers, pots with softened S profile and predominantly simple schemes of horizontal decoration; three varieties can be distinguished: the Corded (B 3) beakers, the Barrel (B 2) beakers and the classic Bell (B 1) beakers shaped like a *campanula* flower. These folk movements started as early as 2000 B.C., on the evidence of radiocarbon analysis in Holland, and were soon followed by others from the Low Countries, bringing the short-necked (C) beakers to Scotland and the North-East. By 1800–1750 B.C. the immigrations were finished and the ensuing spread across Britain probably occupied no more than another hundred years.

Fig. 14

The south-west was remote from the main migration streams and with one exception (the beaker found below the tide mark at Brean Down, Somerset, which is held to be a Breton type, entering by the Bristol Channel) the region received its population late and from insular sources. Two elements can be recognized, first derivatives of the Bell beakers (B 1) of the Wessex chalk, and secondly, a new variety, the long-necked (A) beaker, which, in localities and ways that have yet to be worked out, was evolved in this country probably from a European cordedware prototype. The form, which is widespread in Britain, has a well-marked constriction between the tall splayed neck and rounded body, and in our region is characterised by bold geometric decoration featuring chevron and lozenge patterns.

Plate 13a
BEAKER
BURIALS

Both varieties were in contemporary use in the south-west, as was revealed in the grave mound at Wick, near Stoguersey

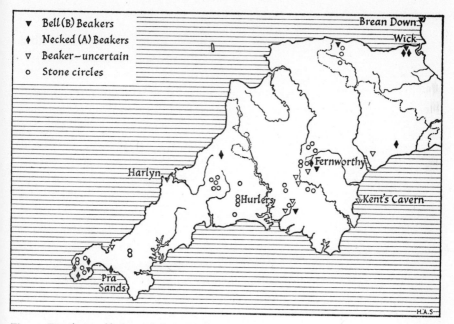

Fig. 14. Distribution of beakers and of stone circles

on the north Somerset coast. This was a large barrow, 90 ft in diameter, 10 ft high, excavated in 1907 by H. St George Gray. The soil casing concealed a walled cairn, 27 ft across, beneath which a number of skeletons had been laid on the old ground surface and which had been disturbed by tomb robbers, surprisingly in Roman times. The three Beaker burials were secondaries, inserted high up in the rubble of the primary cairn. Each was a contracted inhumation, a man with legs tightly drawn up and arms bent; the first was buried with a Bell beaker, the second with a long-necked (A) beaker with chevron decoration and a flint knife-dagger, and the third with a long-necked beaker with lozenge decoration. There can be little doubt that the vessels are approximately contemporary, the products of wide-ranging communities who returned from hunting grounds on the Quantocks to use the barrow built on the coast as their

Plates 12, 13

57

cemetery. The close parallels of the chevron necked (A) beaker with others in the Vale of Glamorgan indicates that some of these people crossed the Channel to colonise the opposite coast.

Fig. 14

The distribution in the south-west shows a concentration in the Land's End peninsula and on Dartmoor, and a scatter on the Bristol Channel coast. The known settlements are coastal, at Praa Sands, Marazion where a long-necked beaker was recovered from a midden, at Gwithian and at Harlyn Bay on the north Cornish coast, and perhaps also at Kent's Cavern, Torbay.

The burials were almost all in cists, just large enough to hold the trussed bodies, as can be seen in the Culbone cist from Exmoor in the Taunton Museum. Some cists are so small, like the 2 ft × 2½ ft stone box on Trevedra Common, St Just, that they can only have held the body of a child or a cremation. The burials were covered by a small round cairn or mound, 12 ft to 20 ft in diameter, rarely more than 2 ft high and inconspicuously sited on moorland slopes.

Their grave-goods were poor and scanty: a bronze blade and a V-perforated lignite button at Fernworthy, barbed and tanged arrowheads at Langcombe and Lakehead, and a bracer at Archerton are all from Dartmoor. The beakers include a few decorative long-necked types, as at Praa Sands, Wick and Fernworthy, but the majority, both A and B derivatives, are debased; there is a tendency to thicken the rim or to add a moulding below it, as in the handled example from Try, Gulval. A date *c.* 1600 B.C., is indicated for most of them.

Plate 14

Plate 15

In their later stages, the Beaker folk in the south-west associated with the makers of the southern type of food-vessel, and adopted the rite of cremation. These food-vessels are unpretentious small pots of biconical form, with bevelled rim and occasional ornament of whipped or twisted cord: it is not clear how they originated in our area, but a secondary Neolithic ancestry may be presumed. Their cultural context is known only from burials. At Broad Down, on the greensand plateau of east Plate 16 Devon, a cremation with a debased necked-beaker was inserted into the edge of a small cairn of flints, which covered a primary cremation in an inverted food-vessel. At Charmy Down, near Bath, an inhumation with a necked-beaker, a bronze knife-dagger, and a ribbed shale bead was contemporary with a cremation in a food-vessel in the centre of a walled cairn like that at Wick, whilst at Cataclews, Harlyn Bay, another food-vessel of this type was associated with a stone battle-axe, a weapon frequently deposited with necked-beakers.

At Tregulland, on Wilsey Down flanking Bodmin Moor, Plate 17 a food-vessel cremation was the last interment in a complex barrow structure, succeeding both the cremation of an archer with two barbed arrowheads, one tanged, one hollow-based, Plate 18 and the primary inhumation, which unfortunately had been thoroughly disturbed. Skilled excavation by Paul Ashbee, however, showed how rich and varied were the funeral rites and customs now developing amongst these peoples. The primary burial was set apart, enclosed by two circles of close-set *Fig. 15* stakes 14 and 24 ft in diameter: the cremation with arrowheads was placed in an elongated grave and fires had been lit in a shallow pit, both just outside the stake circles. The stakes had then been removed and replaced by a cairn-ring, walled internally, and incorporating a number of cup-marked slabs of the Plate 19 local slate. These circular pecked hollows appear to be protective symbols for the Food-Vessel people, analogous to the *occuli* or eye symbols of the Passage Grave people. At Tregulland the food-vessel cremation was placed on the ground within the cairn-ring, and the whole centre was then filled up with soil dug from an encircling ditch, to make a barrow 30 ft in diameter.

The 'single graves' of the Beaker and Food-Vessel peoples STONE ROWS were concealed generally by an inconspicuous small mound. An interesting local development of this very simple funeral

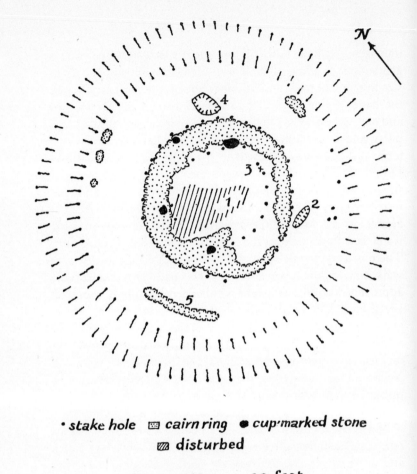

Fig. 15. Plan of Tregulland barrow, Cornwall. 1. disturbed primary burial; 2. cremation grave; 3. food-vessel cremation; 4. 'ritual' pit; 5. remnant of outer kerb

monument occurs on Dartmoor, where some 60 little cairns have settings of rows of stones. A characteristic example is on Watern Down, near the Warren House Inn, where a double row of 50 pairs of granite uprights extends for 180 yards from a transverse terminal slab (the so-called 'blocking stone') up a gentle slope to a low cairn 20 ft in diameter. The stones vary in size from a foot high, just visible in the heather, to nearly 6 feet, the largest being nearest the cairn, as also in the Down Tor and one of the Shovel Down rows. Two shapes are significant, a pillar and a triangular-topped slab; at Merrivale, these two forms are paired as terminals to the southern row; at Shovel Down, they head the row beside the cairn. There is no consistency in the orientation of the alignments, the direction being in nearly every case related to a slope. In several instances, as at Harter on the Meavy, the rows are associated with running water and lead up from the banks of the stream to the cairn. There is usually only space for one person, or at most two, to walk between the rows, and since the small cairn is invariably approached uphill, its height is enhanced because it is seen on a false crest. The alignments thus provide a dignified approach to the burial place.

Plate 20

Plate 21

The cairns usually have a kerb or upright slabs (a peristalith) on their circumference and a central cist. At Shovel Down and Yellowmead, Sheepstor, there are four concentric circles of upright stones within the cairn, perhaps the equivalent of the concentric stake circles discovered at Tregulland.

Fig. 16

Not every row is associated with a cairn: on Headland Warren, Challacombe, three rows converge on a standing stone, and at Merrivale, Princetown, the northern double row has a blocking stone as its terminal. Whether such stones were sacred in themselves like a totem-pole, or whether they mark a burial place, as some menhirs do in Cornwall, has not been ascertained.

Two rows in the Erme Valley are of exceptional length. The row on Butterdon Hill starts from a cairn 35 ft in diameter with a conspicuous peristalith and extends for over a mile along the 1,250 foot hill-top. The Stall Moor row starts from a free-standing stone circle 50 ft in diameter, possibly but not certainly sepulchral in origin, and continues at 1,200 ft for over half a mile before it descends steeply to the river: some of the small stones are covered in blanket peat showing that the mon‑ument was built before the Sub‑Atlantic deterioration of the climate after 900 B.C. Across the river, the alignment continues upstream just above the valley floor for another half‑mile to a tributary, the Red Lake stream whence it can be traced inter‑mittently up the slopes of Greenhill and fading out just before it reaches a small barrow on the crest at 1,550 feet; a distance in all of two and a quarter miles. There is no indication whether the whole thing is one setting or whether two have coalesced.

These long rows must have had a rather different purpose from the general run of stone‑lined paths to the tombs. They are unlikely to mark tribal divisions of grazing, as their course does not follow a natural boundary and their ends are not secured. Contemporary monuments of comparable length are the West Kennet stone avenue linking two sacred sites, Ave‑bury and the Sanctuary, the embanked avenue which leads from Stonehenge to the river Avon, and the long embanked enclosures know as a Cursus at Stonehenge and Gussage Down, Dorset. The function of the Cursus is unknown but an attractive conjecture, originating with the eighteenth century antiquary William Stukeley, is that they mark an arena for funeral games and races. It is conceivable that the long rows on Dartmoor mark a course followed by runners, like those at the Grassmere Fell sports today, or by a religious procession.

SANCTUARIES

Fig. 16
Fig. 17

It is evident that certain places on Dartmoor acquired a special sanctity amongst these people and were used for burials and for ceremonial by several generations. At centres like Shovel Down, Fernworthy, Merrivale or Drizzlecombe, two, three or even four rows with their cairns are associated with other cairns, cists, standing stones *(menhirs)* or with a small‑scale free‑standing circle, the whole group extending over a considerable tract of moorland. It is not unreasonable to assume that the

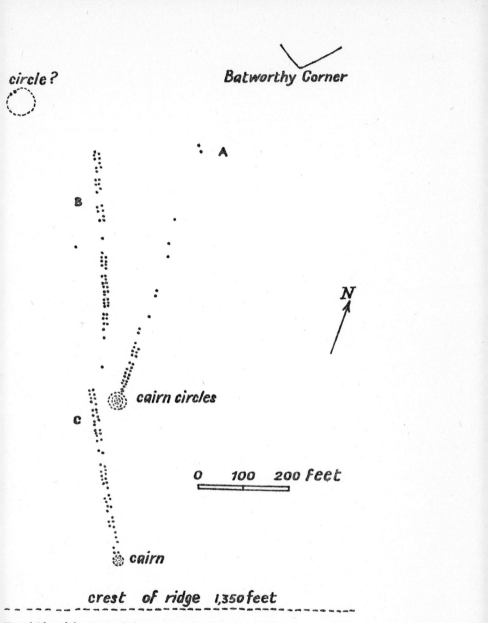

circle ?

Batworthy Corner

A

B

N

cairn circles

C

0   100   200 feet

cairn

crest of ridge 1,350 feet

Fig. 16. Plan of the cairns and alignments on Shovel Down, Chagford, Devon. Row A is over 550 feet long, row B 476 feet, and row C 375 feet

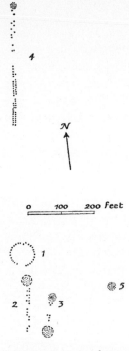

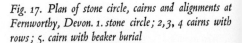

Fig. 17. Plan of stone circle, cairns and alignments at Fernworthy, Devon. 1. stone circle; 2,3, 4 cairns with rows; 5. cairn with beaker burial

Plate 14

monuments in these sanctuaries are, broadly speaking, contem-porary: the few finds are significantly of the Beaker period: a necked beaker from a small cairn at Fernworthy, scraps of another from a cist in the Drizzlecombe group, and a degener-ate Bell beaker from a small cairn near the row on Watern Down. Moreover, the only close parallel in Britain to the Dartmoor rows – the cairn at Garrywhin in Caithness, on which six rows of small stones converge, leading up to it from a nearby stream – contained an inhumation with a cord-ornamented beaker in a cist. Similarly in Holland where the timber equiva-lent to a stone row has been found at Zeijen, in Drenthe, the in-dications are that it is of early Bronze Age date. Here a double line of postholes, 120 ft long and 5 ft wide, begins with a block-ing post and leads to a turf barrow, which covered four inhu-mations and a square mortuary house set within a double circle of posts.

Stone circles were also built independently on the high moor-lands, on Exmoor (3), on Bodmin Moor (9), and on Dartmoor (11); the remainder (7) are in west Cornwall. The majority thus are in districts away from the megalithic tombs and like the stone rows, may be regarded as the religious monuments of Beaker and Food-Vessel people.

The circles are mostly 70 to 80 ft in diameter with stones 4 to 6 ft high as at Tregaseal, St Just. Some, like the Merry Maidens, or Boscawn-un, are true circles with the stones regularly spaced: these must have been set out by a thong from a centre point and the stone holes dug at opposite ends of diagonal intersections. Others, like Stannon on Bodmin Moor, are irregular in outline and in the spacing of the stones. At Boscawn-un and at the Hurlers there is a single upright within the circle, but not at the centre point. The situation chosen is usually on an open stretch of moorland where ceremonials within the circle would have been visible for some distance. The Scorhill circle, for instance, can be seen from the rows on Shovel Down about a mile away.

Plate 22

Plate 23

Once again, sanctity accumulated at these monuments and led to their multiplication. The Grey Wethers, impressively situated on the watershed between the Teign and the East Dart at 1400 feet, consists of a pair of circles 30 feet apart, whilst at the Hurlers, on the south-east flank of Bodmin Moor, there are three circles in a line. The same phenomenon may be noted on Mendip at the four Priddy Rings, which are embanked, and at Stanton Drew, where there are three large stone circles and an alignment that leads to the River Chew. Excavation has thrown little light on the people who built the circles or what they did there. At Fernworthy, Dartmoor, the whole of the interior was found to be covered with charcoal, presumably scattered during a ceremony. At the Hurlers it was discovered that the north and the centre circle were linked by a 6-foot pavé of granite, and that the interior of the north circle was also roughly paved, but there were no finds. The embanked Stripple Stones circle in the middle of Bodmin Moor was excavated by St George Gray in 1907 but nothing was found.

In the absence of dating evidence, we have to fall back on the finds from monuments grouped with the circles, which have already been shown to be Beaker at Fernworthy (p. 64) and which in west Cornwall are Early and Middle Bronze Age barrows as at The Merry Maidens, Rosmodres, or Boske-dan, Gulval. Recent excavations at the Druids' Circle, Pen-maenmawr, in north Wales by W. E. Griffiths, have shown that this 80-foot circle set in a low stony bank was the work of the Food-Vessel people; two children aged 10 to 13, probably sacrifices, had been buried there after cremation and with each was a plain food-vessel of southern type. It seems likely that some circles in the south-west will prove to be of similar origin. On Dartmoor, their number and widespread distribution indicates prolonged use; some were probably not constructed until the Middle Bronze Age.

We perceive in burial and ceremonial sites a difference in religious practice between the megalithic people and the Beaker and Food-Vessel folk. The sanctity of the circle, essentially an open-air monument, has replaced the dark ancestral tomb; within a circle, whether of stakes, stone uprights or cairn-ring, the dead were buried as individuals and honoured by proces-sions or ceremonial visits along a stone-lined path thereafter. Where did these new ideas come from? Probably from southern England, for the best analogy to the monuments lies in the paired stone circles within the great circle at Avebury, or with the double stone setting of the last phase of the Sanctuary on Overton Hill, both linked by the West Kennet alignments and, farther west, with Stanton Drew on the Mendips where stone circles and rows are again combined. Excavation has shown that the Avebury monuments stem from a native (Sec-ondary Neolithic) source, but that it was the Beaker folk who

Fig. 17

Fig. 14

were responsible for their final form; a similar derivation is likely in the south-west.

It has often been suggested that Brittany was the source of the western circles and alignments, but only one pair of circles exists there on the island of Er Lannic in the Gulf of Morbihan, now partly submerged. The many impressive alignments on the Breton mainland are on a far larger scale than anything in south-west England, some using more than 1,000 stones, ar-ranged in ten or more lines and terminating in a semicircular enclosure as at Carnac. They are never associated with burial mounds – indeed, they override a Passage Grave and a long barrow at Manio – and whilst their ceremonial use is not in question, the rites were not connected with an interment.

Finally, the standing stones, or menhirs, which were set up in isolation as well as in the sanctuaries must be considered. These are found throughout the region wherever suitable stone is available, on Exmoor and Dartmoor and are particularly numerous in Cornwall. Many are 10 to 15 ft high and their transport and erection shows great skill. The tallest was Maen Pearn, Constantine, 24 ft high, but it was broken up in the 18th century. The stones have been carefully selected but do not appear to have been dressed; excavation has shown that they were slid into a prepared stone hole and trigged up by a packing of small stones.

MENHIRS

In the Land's End peninsula, several were associated with burials. At Try in Gulval parish, a handled beaker was buried in a small cist three feet away from the base of a tall menhir, together with the long-bones and some cremated human frag-ments. At Trevennack, Paul, a large handled Middle Bronze Age urn containing a cremation was deposited in a pit two feet away from the $11\frac{1}{2}$-feet tall menhir and a small lugged pot placed a little farther off. Deposits of cremated bones and char-red wood are also recorded at the base of three others, at Trelew and Penrhyn in St Buryan parish and also at Trenuggo in

Plate 15

Sancreed. At Kerrow, Zennor a rather different practice was
observed; two pots of Middle or Late Bronze Age type were
placed one inside the other, on a heap of charcoal, and buried
under a layer of stones at the foot of the menphir: they probably
contained offerings of food or drink since no bones were found.
The two tall stones known as the Pipers near the Merry Maidens
circle, Rosmodres, however, had nothing beside them, nor had
a menhir on St Breock's Down recently investigated; such
stones may have been cult objects, like the stones on Easter
Island. Such evidence as there is again indicates that their erec
tion started in Beaker times, and continued well into the Middle
Bronze Age, that is from 1600–1000 B.C.

The foregoing chapters have made it clear that although we
know so little about their domestic life, there was much variety
in the peoples inhabiting the south-western peninsula. About
1600–1500 B.C., an enterprising trader on his travels by sea-ways
and ridgeways might encounter some groups of Western Neolithic stock erecting a chamber-tomb in Penwith, others inserting
yet one more cremation burial into an Entrance Grave, or
Beaker tribesmen bringing their dead chief for interment in a
small cist with his possessions. Other communities as at Tregulland had different funeral rites, involving the setting out of
stake circles, and the cutting of protective symbols on the cairn
stones. At the sanctuaries on Dartmoor, he might see ceremonies in stone circles or at the raising of a long stone, as well
as processions up and down the alignments to the little stone-
ringed cairns covering the graves. Both inhumation and cremation were practised. Stone remained the normal material for
tools and weapons; only a few of the Beaker chieftains had
been able to acquire a small copper or bronze blade. Polished
stone axes and the new holed battle-axe continued to be made
from the local greenstones, but their export to Wessex was
coming to an end.

We have now to see how a more uniform society developed
in the ensuing Bronze Age.

CHAPTER V

Prospectors and Traders
of the Early Bronze Age

THE QUICKENING OF LIFE in the south-west in the middle of the second millennium B.C., with its resultant changes in settlement and burial customs which we shall examine in this and the next chapter, was due to a stimulus from overseas which affected the whole of southern Britain. Actual immigrants were apparently few, the main object being the opening-up of new sources of metal, and trade in raw materials and in finished goods. In Wessex, in particular, a rich civilisation developed, manifest in the numerous and varied possessions buried with the dead – bronze daggers, flat axes, amber and faience beads, gold ornaments, bronze pins – showing contacts with the metalliferous regions of central Europe on the one hand, and with Eire on the other, and through intermediaries, with the Mycenaean civilisation of the Mediterranean. A similar development occurred in Brittany at the same time, shown in the Armorican dagger graves. It might be expected that the south-west, with its rich supply of alluvial tin and with some accessible copper (p. 21), would have shared in this florescence, but whilst some outstanding exotic objects were brought here at the outset and in the course of trade, the Early Bronze Age civilisation that developed pales in comparison with that farther east. This is probably because the land was relatively thinly populated by the Neolithic and Beaker races, and the inhabitants were exploited by the metal merchants.

Fig. 2

In Wessex two phases can be distinguished, the first from *c.* 1600–1550 B.C. being marked by extended inhumation burials under round barrows with triangular copper or bronze daggers with six rivets, the second, starting 1550–1500 B.C. by

INHUMATION
BURIALS

predominantly cremation burials with ogival grooved daggers. The early phase is scarcely represented in the south-west, although a find in one of the richest of the Wessex chieftain's graves, Bush Barrow near Stonehenge, shows that contacts existed. This is the perforated stone macehead which is a pebble of Devonian limestone from the Teignmouth district: together with the remarkable bronze-bound wand or sceptre which has affinities in the Mycenaean shaft-graves (and to which the macehead was formerly held to belong) it was probably part of royal insignia.

One outstanding chieftain's burial is in the early Wessex manner, the extended skeleton in a long stone cist in the Rillaton barrow, Linkinhorne, in east Cornwall. The burial place overlooks the rich mineral deposits of Caradon, south-east of Bodmin Moor, and is accessible by ridgeway from St Germans estuary, a western branch of Plymouth Sound. The position of the cist high up in the side of the 120 foot round mound of turf and stone shows that the burial must be a secondary: the grave-goods indicate that he may well be a direct descendant of a prospector. With the corpse was a corrugated gold cup, an ogival dagger, some 'pieces of ivory (bone?), glass (faience?) beads and pottery', now all lost.

The fine gold cup, $3\frac{1}{4}$ inches high, is unique: the horizontal ribbing, and the ribbon-like handle, margined with chased lines and secured by three rivets and diamond-shaped washers, are features that link it with products of Aegean metalworkers. It resembles a pair of small ribbed gold cups from shaft-grave IV, one of the royal tombs in the grave-circle at Mycenae, dating from the sixteenth century B.C. The profile at first glance is reminiscent of a Bell beaker but in reality it is a softened version of a biconical form which we shall meet again in shale at Farway, or in the gold cup from Fritzdorf, Bonn, which in turn was inspired by Mycenaean shaft-grave models. The Rillaton cup was probably an heirloom when it was placed in the

Fig. 22

Plate 24

Plate 25

grave with the ogival dagger, and the glass or faience beads in the late fifteenth century B.C.

At East Putford in North Devon, an extended inhumation, totally decayed, and with traces of a corroded bronze blade and a wooden pole beside it was buried in a rectangular timber mortuary house, beneath a ditched round barrow of turf. The structure measured 6 ft by 4 ft between the angle posts and was thought by the excavator, C. A. R. Radford, to be gabled and 3 ft high; the top was covered by stones and burnt clay. This too could be the interment of an early Bronze Age chieftain.

There are other massive cists in the peninsula which are large enough to have held an extended inhumation, such as those on Dartmoor at Merrivale and Roundy Park or in Longridge Wood, Roadwater, in Somerset, but there is no record of their contents. At Botrea Hill, Sancreed, although no bones were found, two fine ovate barbed and tanged arrowheads were recovered like those found in the early series of Breton dagger graves, whilst on the cliffs at Trevelgue a handsome boat-shaped stone battle-axe, resembling others found in some early Wessex graves was associated with a contracted skeleton in a large cist.

After 1500 B.C., contemporary with the second phase in Wessex, the picture is fuller and better defined: we have, on the one hand, a widespread distribution of cremation burials with ogival daggers, necklaces and small cups of pottery or shale and, in Cornwall, with ribbon-handled urns, and on the other the introduction of the conspicuously-sited large round barrow or cairn, some of unusual form, and often massed in an extensive cemetery. Information about settlement and domestic life, however, is still lacking.

The changes are best seen in the Farway necropolis on the Greensand in east Devon, where some 50–60 barrows are concentrated on a narrow ridge that divides the head of the rivers Sid and Coly at a focal point in the hill system and traffic ways. Re-examination of the accounts left by the nineteenth century

CREMATION
CEMETERIES

Fig. 21

71

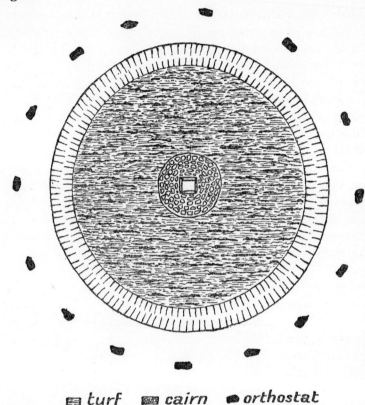

🝙 *turf*   🝙 *cairn*   ◕ *orthostat*

Fig. 18. Barrow with stone circle surround and ditch, Farway east Devon

antiquaries, R. Kirwan and P. O. Hutchinson, show that the burials began with cremations by Food‑Vessel and belated Beaker folk in a small flint cairn. The next stage was the erec‑ tion of large turf mounds, 80–140 ft in diameter, 6–12 ft high, some ditched, some surrounded by a free‑standing stone circle; these covered cremations which were placed either on a pave‑ ment or in a cist beneath a primary flint cairn. The grave‑goods were of types new to the area: a grooved dagger, Kimmeridge

Plate 16

Fig. 18

shale cups and pottery, and a segmented bone bead, a form copied from imported faience, but perforated transversely so that it could be used as a toggle.

The cups are fine examples of Early Bronze Age craftsman-ship, carved out of soft dark shales from the Kimmeridge beds in south Dorset or from the very similar lignites of the Bovey beds in south Devon. The bases are rounded and it is likely that they were finished by turning on a pole lathe against a flint blade; if so, this is the earliest known instance of turning in Britain. The form is copied from a metal prototype ultimately of Aegean origin and well exemplified in the Fritzdorf gold cup, whilst the decoration on the handle of the best example is the same as on the Rillaton gold cup. Similar cups in shale and translucent Baltic amber are among the princely appurtenances in rich Wessex graves as at Clandon, Dorset, with a sceptre, and at Hove, Sussex, with a stone battle-axe. At Farway, both cups were found close to the cremation and so may have been used to pour a final libation. The pottery pygmy cup on the other hand contained the burnt bones of an infant: the two perforations are 'eyes', *oculi*, the protective symbol of the mega-lithic mother-goddess, well known from the Folkton chalk idols (or 'drums') from Yorkshire.

Plates 25, 26

Plate 24

Plate 27

The new aristocratic element in society is evident also from the arrangement of some of the barrows at Farway: seven of them are set in a row on the edge of the plateau, suggesting that this part of the cemetery was reserved for successive burials of a dynasty. The central mound, which contained a dagger and a shale cup, was the largest; it was probably the first chief-tain's burial place. The blending of old and new in burial custom and hence, it can be inferred, in population is shown by the small stone circles of Beaker origin which surrounded two of the mounds. Finally, it can be perceived that these people brought their dead to the cemetery from a wide area and over a long period of time, for the Greensand plateau, uniformly

Fig. 18

suitable for settlement, is destitute of barrows for many miles around.

Another cemetery of twenty large mounds is in the lower Exe valley situated on a patch of well-drained alluvial soils on either side of the river, near Bramford Speke. Typical early grave-goods were found in 1869 in a barrow on Stevenstone farm, a small grooved dagger, a pottery cup and a necklace, wrapped up with cremated bones in a skin or cloth and fastened with a bronze spiral pin. The eyed pygmy cup was decorated with twisted cord, and the tiny oblate shale beads and an encrinite (the fossilised stem of a plant) were probably chosen for the necklace because they resembled the shape of imported segmented faience beads.

A cemetery of ten barrows near Pelynt, south Cornwall also belongs to this early Bronze Age phase; the barrows, which were excavated in 1830–45, contained cremations, one with an ogival dagger, another with a greenstone macehead, and with a third was the famous short sword or dagger of late Mycenaean type. As Professor Gordon Childe pointed out in 1951, this square-shouldered weapon with a flanged hilt plate must have been made in the Aegean, perhaps as early as the fourteenth or thirteenth century B.C., though the closest analogies are the short swords from a tomb at Diakata, Kephallenia, which have been dated to the twelfth century. The Pelynt find is of great importance because it substantiates the recognition of another Mycenaean dagger – an earlier type resembling those in the sixteenth century shaft-grave VI at Mycenae – which is carved on one of the sarsen uprights at Stonehenge.

Other cemeteries with early grave-goods in Devon are Huntshaw Cross, Torrington, with a large ogival dagger, and Halwill where an amber pendant of Wessex type was recorded. The occasional bell and disc barrows in some cemeteries as on the Taphouse ridge above the River Fowey, and among the Five Barrows (actually eight) on Exmoor, are also significant, for

Plate 28

Plate 35

Plate 31

Plate 53

these forms, in which the burial place is isolated by a berm and surrounded by a ditch and an external bank, are peculiar to early Bronze Age burials in Wessex.

It is already apparent that there was no uniformity in the deposition of the dead nor in the barrow construction in the cemeteries, and the same is true of isolated burials. At North Molton, north Devon, a cremation with a necklace of imported blue faience beads and other grave-goods (lost) was simply placed in a cist under a small mound. At Hameldon, 1700 ft up on the eastern flank of Dartmoor, the cremation with a grooved dagger having an amber pommel decorated with gold pins *(pointillé)* was deposited under a slab pavement but not in the centre of the mound. This was occupied by a small cairn, covering a primary ritual deposit, and the whole enclosed by a circular stone wall or cairn-ring, and finally concealed by a mound of peaty turf 40 feet in diameter. Two other barrows further north on the same ridge, Single Barrow and Broad Barrow, are known to be similarly constructed and presumably were erected for the same dynasty.

The Hameldon dagger pommel is a remarkable piece; the form and cruciform decoration show it to be a copy of a well-know Early Bronze Age weapon in southern and central Europe; its pointillé technique can be matched on bone or wooden hilts of daggers in Wessex and Brittany. To reproduce it in amber was a technical *tour de force*, involving the drilling of hundreds of tiny close set holes for the insertion of gold wire pins; moreover, the pommel was broken and a repair attempted by rabbeting on the piece and securing the edges of the join with seven more pins widely spaced. Like the Farway shale cups, it indicates that there were craftsmen of a very high order in the area capable of effecting such a repair for what was presumably originally an imported piece. It suggests, as does the Rillaton cup, that some of the early prospectors bringing splendid gifts explored the estuaries along the southern coast,

Plate 35

Plate 33

Fig. 19

Fig. 20

Plate 33

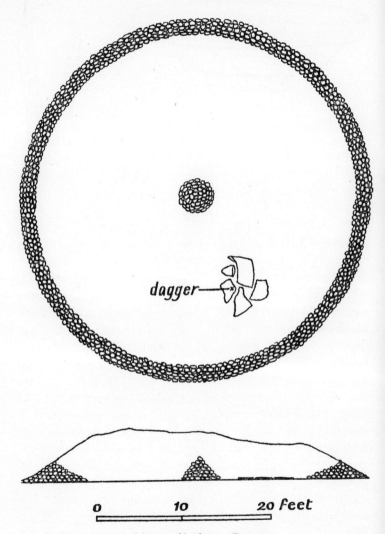

dagger

Fig. 19. *Plan and section of the Hameldon barrow, Dartmoor*

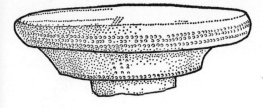

Fig. 20. The Hameldon dagger, an amber pommel decorated with gold pins and a bronze blade. Width of pommel 2¼ in., length of blade 4 in

and succeeded in establishing themselves in the metalliferous districts of the hinterland.

In Cornwall, cremation burials with ogival daggers and other grave-goods are in another mode, in which the bones were collected and placed in a large ribbon-handled urn. These handsome vessels are biconical, tall, wide-mouthed and tapering to a small base: they are named from the pair of broad loop handles which are applied to the widest part of the urn and through which thongs could be passed for lifting or tilting the pot. The manufacture from the local clays and subsequent firing of these large vessels on an open hearth represent a considerable technical achievement. They are heavily ornamented with impressed cord patterns on both sides of the bevelled rim, and on the neck and handles. The decoration is carefully done, giving an impression either of a plait of three strands, rather like an ear of wheat or a classical laurel wreath, or else of a firm double twist. A typical burial is that in a barrow at Blood Hound Cove, within the sheltered Harlyn Bay on the Cornish coast: with the 20 in. high urn was a grooved dagger, a little whetstone for sharpening it and an eyed pygmy cup like that

RIBBON-HANDLED URN-BURIALS

Plates 36, 37

77

Plate 55

Plate 36

Fig. 21

from Stevenstone, Devon. At Crig-a-Mennis, Perranzabuloe, a magnificent urn – one of two found in the recently excavated barrow (p. 107) – contained a plain pygmy cup and some clay beads. In all, four surviving urns have been found with grooved daggers, five with other grave-goods including faience beads at Carn Creis, and there are 13 unaccompanied urns, such as that from a cist at Tregaseal, St Just, which was contemporary with an Entrance Grave. Since fragments have been found in Middle Bronze Age settlements at Trevisker, and Gwithian (layer 7) and in the Ash Hole cave at Brixham, the urns had a domestic use, probably as grain storage jars.

The distribution affects both north and south Cornish coasts; there is no marked concentration in Penwith where the mega-lithic peoples must have remained strongly entrenched; only later in the Middle Bronze Age when the form and decoration of the urns were modified (Group 2 on p.85, Patchett's Class C) did their makers dominate Land's End. In Devon the early form of urn is rare. Outliers in Wessex are of interest as they indicate contacts from 1400 B.C. onwards: the earliest is the Winterslow urn with plaited cord decoration which was a secondary burial in a Bell-barrow above a primary Bell-beaker interment: with the urn were a tanged razor (Class I), am-ber beads, and a pygmy cup. Handled urns from Hengist-bury Head, Lord's Down, Dewlish, and other places in south Dorset indicate that some Cornish folk also settled west of the Stour in the Middle Bronze Age. This small-scale movement had important effects on the development of later Bronze Age ceramics in Wessex, including the globular urn.

It must now be considered whether these distinctive and novel pots are the products of an invasion or whether they are native to the south-west. It used to be thought that they were intrusive and of Breton origin, analogous to the handled bico-nical pots found in the second series of the Armorican dagger graves. The differences are that the handles of the Breton pots

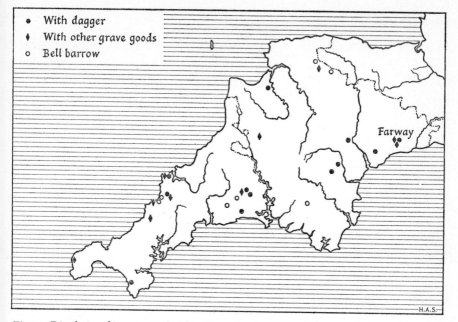

Farway

H.A.S.

Fig. 21. Distribution of Bronze Age burials with grave-goods of Wessex type

are placed below the rim, not on the girth, they are normally four, not two, and the ornament, when it occurs, is grooved or incised, not corded. Because of these differences, Mr A. ApSimon has recently suggested that prototypes are to be sought in the globular corded amphorae of late Neolithic times in Saxo-Thuringia, which have lug handles on the girth. He sees the Cornish urns as products of immigrants of east German descent coming from the Rhineland and responsible also for the introduction of ogival daggers and for trade contacts with Wessex. It must, however, be admitted that the continental pots are not like the Cornish urns in shape, nor in their scheme of decoration, and that they were produced 200 or 300 years earlier. In favour of native development it can be urged that biconical pots, some with lugs, were used by the Megalithic peoples, as at Knackyboy or Zennor, that decorated handles were made by Beaker folk at Try, and that the Food-Vessel people at

Plate 9
Plate 15

Farway were acquainted with twisted cord ornament. The decorated ribbon-handles of the exotic Rillaton and Farway cups
could also be related to these urns. At the present state of
knowledge no final conclusion can be reached.

Broadly speaking, it is evident that the south-western peninsula formed a cultural province in the early Bronze Age analogous to, and contemporary with, the second phase of the Wessex culture of southern Britain. Within the area, there were
regional differences; the peoples in east Devon, the Exe valley
and probably in west Somerset were related to those in Dorset
and Wiltshire, whilst those farther west developed different pottery and burial rites. It can hardly be a coincidence that the
megalithic colonisation was limited to those western areas and
as we have seen, some Penwith and Scillonian tombs were
still being used at this time.

The lure of metals, of copper and above all tin, was the attrac-
tion that brought the prospectors and traders down the English
Channel across the Irish sea, or up the Atlantic coast. Eire had
an abundant supply of copper and gold in the Wicklow and
Kerry hills, but once it was known that the addition of 10%
of tin improved the cutting edge of copper, converting it into
bronze, her merchant-smiths had to come to Cornwall and
Devon for their supplies. The gifts they proffered in exchange
for the black cassiterite pebbles were flat axes and gold insignia,
(lunulae). One of the earliest imports is a long thin axe with a
characteristic square butt, from Drewsteignton in the Teign
valley; later came the round-heeled axes with flanges and crescentic blades decorated with incised geometric patterns found
at St Erth, St Blazey and Sidmouth. The *lunulae* are crescents
of gold beaten thin to the consistency of stiffened linen and worn
as bibs, or less likely, collars; their decoration of finely chased
geometric patterns is a translation into linear design of the
crescentic necklaces of amber or jet found in Wessex and in
northern England. A pair of *lunulae* were found with a plain

Plates 24, 25

TRADE AND
METALWORK,
IRISH

Fig. 22

Plates 29, 30

80

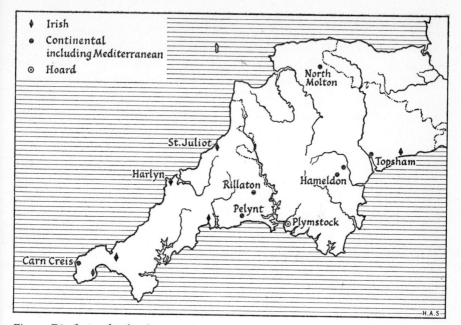

Fig. 22. Distribution of Irish and continental Bronze Age imports

Plate 32

flat axe on the coast at Harlyn in 1865, another on Cargurra Farm, Hennet, St Juliot and a third near Gulval, all within reach of sheltered sandy beaches and the tin streams.

The evidence for tin working at this time is a dagger (lost) from a tin stream at St Ewe, and what can be deduced from exports. There is the remarkable little necklace from Odoorne found in the peat in the province of Drenthe, north Holland, which has 25 beads of tin strung with 4 of segmented faience, and 14 of amber. Farther east in Denmark there are the handled wooden bowls from burials in oak coffins of the early Bronze Age as Guldhoj, Jutland: these resemble the amber cup from Hove in shape but are decorated *en pointillé* with rows of tin nails round the body and a cross on the base. Their position near the amber coasts and in a region where Irish exports – *lunulae*, decorated axes and halberds – have been found must indicate that the Irish merchant-smiths were the intermediaries in the overseas tin trade.

The peoples in Wessex also needed tin and copper for the manufacture of ogival daggers and the newer types of flanged axes: a segmented bead of tin from Sutton Veney, Wilts (lost) shows that the Cornish metal was being exported in the fourteenth century. It is clear from analysis that some copper, with a characteristic high nickel content, was obtained by Wessex from the continent: at present copper of south-western origin can not be distinguished from Irish metal since both have a high arsenical impurity, and so its exploitation remains uncertain. The large bronze hoard found under a stone at Orston Point, Plymstock, on the estuary of the Plym in 1869 must represent the stock in trade of a merchant-smith, who came from Wessex at this time. It consisted of 16 flanged axes, 3 ogival daggers, a tanged spearhead and a punch or chisel, of which recent analysis has shown that they have a high nickel content. Such finished goods could be exchanged for tin obtainable in the upper reaches of the river on Dartmoor.

Fig. 22

MEDITERRA-
NEAN TRADE

Plate 35

We have already seen that in the sixteenth and fifteenth centuries B.C., imports of Mycenaean inspiration reached the south-west, which had filtered through from central European sources (p. 70). During the fourteenth century the traders brought segmented blue faience beads, manufactured in the eastern Mediterranean. These appear in tombs of the XVIIIth dynasty at Abydos in Egypt and at Lachish in Palestine, dating between 1450 and 1370 B.C., as well as in late Mycenaean tombs at Thapsos in Sicily and on Lipari. The distribution indicates that there were two routes from the Mediterranean; a central European route by the Danube to the centres of the Aunjetitz culture in Moravia, and thence by the Rhine to the North Sea, and a western route across southern France by the Garonne to the Atlantic and thence by sea to Brittany. The beads found at Knackyboy in the Scillies, Carn Creis in Penwith, and North

Fig. 22
Plate 35

Molton, Devon, presumably reached the peninsula by the western route, since the bicone beads on the North Molton necklace can be matched at Kerstrobel in Brittany. The traders who thus entered North Devon from the Bristol channel went on to bring segmented beads to Bronze Age people on the Mendips, at Blackdown and Priddy. On the south coast a lost necklace from Moor Barton in the Teign valley, south Devon, may have come by the central European route with the consignments of beads to Wessex.

Plate 31
Plate 34

Sporadic Mediterranean imports occur on the south coast at a later date. As well as the sub-Mycenaean dagger from Pelynt (p. 74) there is a double-axe of 94% copper from Mount Howe, Topsham, on the Exe estuary. This with its characteristic oval shaft-hole was undoubtedly made in the Aegean: its closest analogies are in hoards on the Acropolis at Athens and in the late Poros wall area at Mycenae, both dating *c.* 1250 B.C. The imports of bronze pins and other objects from the Aunjetitz people which occur in some of the later graves in Wessex and also at Camerton, south of Bath, in Somerset, do not appear in the south-western peninsula: it may well be that during the thirteenth century overseas contacts were solely by the Atlantic route.

Chapter VI

South-Western Bronze Age
Societies

There is no doubt that the centuries from 1500–1300 B.C. were the formative period in Bronze Age culture and society throughout the south-west. It was, as we have seen, a period of stimulus from overseas trading contacts, from which followed the welding together of the mixed late Neolithic, Beaker and Food Vessel stocks under new leaders, some being immigrants in the first place, others appearing no doubt in response to the challenge of the times. This epoch was succeeded by a long period of relative stability, from 1300–450 B.C., or even later in some districts, when there was no radical change in the population or in their way of life. During this period there was a steady increase in the population shown by the number and size of the settlements with their associated fields and stock enclosures and by the multiplication and spread of barrow burials, until in certain areas like Dartmoor the habitable land must have been fully taken up.

CHRONOLOGY

The difficulty of this long period, until very recently, has been its lack of fixed points to which to attach a chronology. Weapons and ornaments, which are dateable, now ceased to be placed in the graves and owing to the acid soil have not survived in the settlements on the granite. The excavations of numerous huts which took place in the late nineteenth and early twentieth centuries were unskilfully conducted and inadequately recorded; consequently no sequence of stratified pottery was established and the whole issue bedevilled by the wishful thinking of the local antiquaries who had proclaimed that everything was 'Early Bronze Age' or 'Neolithic'. Nor were the domestic wares, mostly found in Devon, correlated with fune-rary urns, mostly found in Cornwall: apparent differences were emphasised and likenesses overlooked so that the essential cultural unity of the peninsula remained unappreciated.

Excavations in the post-war period have changed this situa-tion. In Cornwall, sherds of ribbon-handled urns have been found in huts at Trevisker, St Eval, enabling Mr A. ApSimon to work out a sequence of pottery styles starting in the early Middle Bronze Age, and to correlate it with the development of the funeral urns. At Gwithian, an open settlement on the dunes flanking the Hayle estuary, Mr Charles Thomas has obtained a stratified sequence with three layers of Bronze Age occupation separated by blown sand. The last of these (layer 3) was dated by two bronze pins with south German affinities to the period 1300-1100 B.C. and by a mould of local stone for an early form of socketed axe, the north-east German type which occurs in the Bishopland and Taunton hoards, and which is dated *circa* 1000-900 B.C. From Dartmoor, pottery has been obtained from an enclosed settlement on Dean Moor, Avon valley, which can be placed in the Cornish sequence, whilst at Kestor, Chagford, an iron smelting furnace in a hut showed that the culture survived till at least 450 B.C.

Pottery is now the key to a new chronology. It falls into three stylistic groups, developing one from the other at Trevisker, and successively stratified at Gwithian.

POTTERY

(1) The early group is characterised by cord ornament, prin-cipally the laureate plait: it includes the biconical ribbon-handled pots previously described (p. 77) and dates from the second Wessex phase, *c.* 1400 B.C. (Trevisker style 1).

Plates 36, 37

(2) In the middle group, cord ornament continues but twisted impressions now predominate. There is much incised or groov-ed decoration done with a rounded point and some prodding.

85

Plate 38

'Dimple' impressions, cruciform 'ribs' of applied clay on the base, and flat cordons on the body now appear: loop and lug handles continue. The large pots are either rounded or straight-sided; most rims have an internal bevel, occasionally they are everted. (Trevisker styles 2 and 3; Gwithian layer 5).

(3) In the late group, cord ornament has died out; incised patterns continue, either narrow scratched lines at Gwithian, or untidy broad ones on Dartmoor. Square lugs and flat cordons

Plates 40, 41

continue on straight-sided and globular pots: rims are flat-topped, tapering to body, or have an internal bevel (Trevisker style 4; Gwithian layer 3, dated 1200–900 B.C.).

In Cornwall the later wares are harder and better fired: in Devon there is no change until the introduction of Iron Age 'A' ceramic with everted rims, carination and fingertip ornament as at Kestor, Foales Arrishes and Dainton.

SETTLEMENTS

The study of pottery styles, however, is only a means to an end; it enables us to arrange settlements and burials chronologically so that the stages by which man came to terms with his environment can be ascertained. Broadly speaking, there are two ways of getting a living from the land, by arable cultivation and by stock-keeping: both were practised by the Bronze Age peoples, not exclusively but in varying proportion by different groups. It is these differences in economy, not in chronology, that define the settlement types.

PASTORAL

First the pastoralists: these lived in enclosed and/or nucleated settlements surviving principally on Dartmoor and Bodmin. The walls of the enclosures are substantial, built with a facing of granite boulders and a core of small stones, 7–9 ft thick and probably 6–8 ft high. Inside there are usually five to ten scattered round huts, but sometimes as many as twenty to thirty; single huts are rare. There may also be stock-pens attached to the

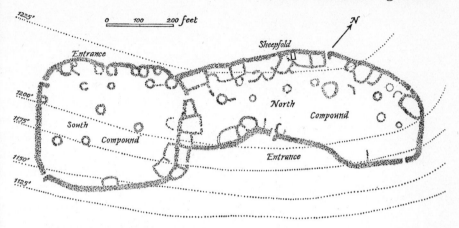

Fig. 23. Plan of Rider's Rings enclosed settlement, Dartmoor

main wall, as at Rider's Rings in the Avon valley. On Dart-   *Fig. 23*
moor these settlements are distributed thickly on the southern   *Fig. 24*
and western valleys, on the south-facing slopes between 1000
and 1300 ft. Their relation to water and to good grazing is obvious, as on the Avon where groups of settlements occupy
successive tracts of moorland divided by tributary streams. The
Legis Tor settlements are built at the edge of the River Plym
whilst Grimspound, Manaton, which lies in a fold in the hills   *Plate 46*
between Hameldon and Hookney Tor, is sited on a small
stream, the Grims Lake which flows under the wall.

Indications that there was cultivation in the enclosure are
rare. Soil washes downhill naturally after heavy rain particularly
if it has been trampled by cattle, and in piling up behind the
wall on the lower side has a deceptive appearance of a lynchet,
as at Trowlesworthy. At Riders Rings there are some sub-   *Fig. 23*
rectangular walled plots in the centre of the double enclosure,
which look like cultivation patches, and elsewhere the placing
of huts only on the perimeter of an enclosure is suggestive. A
broken saddle-quern and rubbers at Dean Moor in the Avon

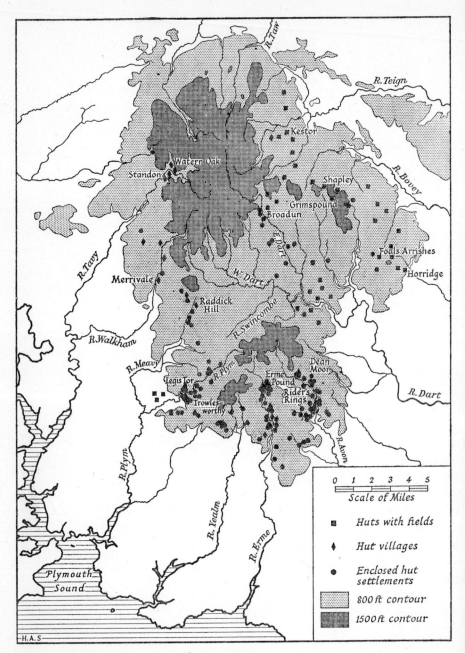

Fig. 24. *Distribution of Bronze Age settlements on Dartmoor*

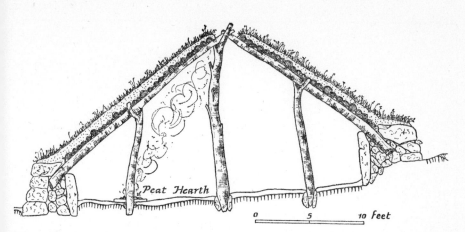

Fig. 25. Reconstructed section of a Dartmoor hut at Kestor, Chagford, Devon

valley shows that some grain was grown but the cultivation
plots were not located.

There are also open village settlements in which the huts are
linked by low walls forming irregular enclosures, that could
be used for cultivation or for stock. Some of these settlements
are very large, for example 68 huts on Standon Down, and 94
at Watern Oke, both in the upper Tavy valley, and there are
similar settlements on Bodmin Moor, as at Rough Tor. Their
layout indicates a mixed economy, predominantly pastoral.

The huts are circular, varying from 10–25 ft in internal diameter, with walls 4–5 ft thick and of the same height. They were
entered by a narrow doorway, which faced away from the
piercing north-west wind, and sometimes screened by a curved
wall forming a sort of vestibule as at Grimspound. Excavation
at Dean Moor has shown that their conical thatched roof was
supported on a central upright post and a ring of 6 or 7 others,
3 or 4 ft away from the hut wall. The principal rafters rested
on these and on the wall-top, wedged amongst the large stones,
and converged at the apex where they could be secured to the
centre post. Lighter timbers would be fastened to the rafters,
and the remaining space filled with supple hazel or alder

Fig. 24

Plate 42

branches, as a foundation for a reed or heather thatch. Looking upwards in the gloom inside the hut, the roof structure would look like a spider's web, with a hole in the centre for the smoke to escape. In the smaller huts in settlements like Grimspound, the roof was constructed wig-wam fashion without internal supports.

The large circular hut with an interior post-ring has a long life in this region: it begins at Trevisker and Dean Moor in the Middle Bronze Age and occurs in an irregular oval form at Gwithian (p. 94) about 1300 B.C. It persists throughout the Iron Age as at Kestor, at Bodrifty and at Castle Dore hill-fort. During the Roman period, it was superseded by less regular settings of posts, and sub-rectangular forms begin to appear as in the courtyard houses (p. 148).

Fig. 25

Fig. 26

At Dean Moor, the evolution of an interior house plan is perceptible. The lower side of the hut was the kitchen and working-quarters: the hearth was here, edged with small stones and nearby were several small pits or holes, 1–2 ft deep, in which food was cooked by covering it with hot ash or with heated river pebbles. At Raddick Hill on the Meavy and at Legis Tor on the Plym, whole pots were found sunk in such holes, presumably to prevent upset, and to keep their contents cool. The upper part of the floor, which was levelled into the hillside, was relatively clean and in two huts was separated by a setting of boulders (Hut 2) or by a low wall (Hut 8) to form an inner room, the sleeping quarters. In Hut 5A, one of two huts that can only be called semi-detached, this clean floor extended to form a recess 5 ft 3 in. by 4 ft, which may be compared with the 'neuks' for box-beds surviving in some Orkney crofts today. These developments from the primitive open house plan, which has become fashionable again in the mid-twentieth century, show the beginnings of a desire for privacy and imply a change in late Bronze Age society away from the communal habitation.

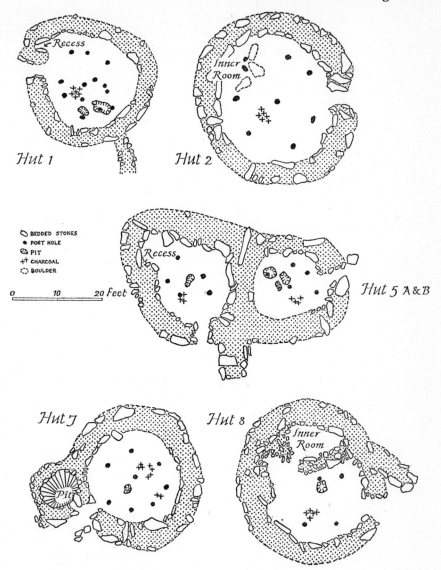

Fig. 26. Hut types in the Dean Moor enclosed settlement, Dartmoor

Plates 38, 41

Pottery from the Dartmoor pastoral settlements belongs to the middle and late groups: the pots from Raddick Hill and the Dewerstone are representative.

ARABLE

Fig. 27

The arable settlements are open with the dwellings placed on the edges of the fields, or a yard as at the Rippon Tor homestead on Dartmoor. Two to four huts with six to eight fields make up a small settlement, and represent the holding of a family group. The fields, which are lynchetted, are small, one third to half an acre: they are edged by a row of granite slabs and boulders which have been cleared off before ploughing, and sometimes reinforced by a packing of small stones and soil: at Gwithian, in west Cornwall, there was some evidence that thorny brushwood had been used for a similar purpose. The fields are normally rectilinear and squarish, a shape suitable for cross ploughing.

Plate 43

At Gwithian the actual plough marks have been preserved: they show up either as brown bands of humic soil in a base of yellow sand, or where the last furrows have been filled by blown sand, as yellow stripes on a brown soil-base. The furrows are 3–4 in. deep, V shaped with one side vertical and one oblique, widely spaced from 1 ft to 2 ft apart and they cross and intersect, showing clearly that the field was ploughed both ways, as advocated by Vergil in the *Georgics* (I: 97). These marks were produced by a light wooden plough, a 'crook ard', made from a bent bough with the tip hardened for the share by charring: such ploughs are depicted drawn by oxen on Bronze Age rock carvings at Monte Bego in the Alpes Maritimes and have been found in peat bogs in Jutland dating from the Iron Age. Places on the edges of the fields where the plough

Plate 44

could not reach were dug over with a spade at Gwithian, which left D shaped marks, 4–5 in. deep, similar to those made by a long-handled shovel with a pointed blade such as is used in Cornwall and west Wales today. This and the spacing of the furrows wide enough for a man to walk between, indicates

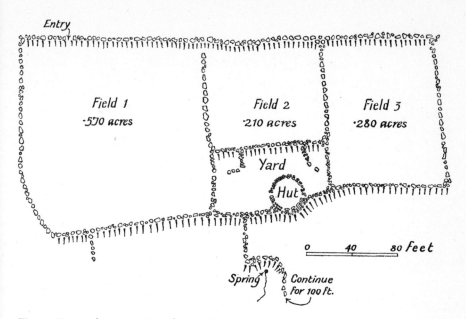

Entry

Field 1
·570 acres

Field 2
·210 acres

Field 3
·280 acres

Yard

Hut

Spring
Continue
for 100 ft.

0   40   80 Feet

Fig. 27. Homestead at Rippon Tor, Ilsington, Dartmoor

careful husbandry. Barley, both naked and hulled varieties, was grown on the evidence of impressions on Cornish Middle Bronze Age pottery.

On Dartmoor some family holdings expanded and multiplied until their fields coalesced, and extended over nearly a mile of moorland, as at Kestor, Foales Arrishes or Horridge. The original field pattern often has been altered by medieval cultivators combining several fields into a long strip. There are droveways between the field-walls to the open moor, showing that grazing was an essential part of the economy.

The distribution of the agriculturalists is complementary to that of the pastoralists, being concentrated on the eastern side of Dartmoor, with a small overlap only in the valleys of the East Dart and Plym. The explanation is geographical: the eastern side has a considerably lower rainfall and therefore is

Plate 47

Fig. 24

better suited to cereal cultivation. It follows that the settlement types are, broadly speaking, contemporary and belong to the same people or culture.

The huts in the arable settlements are noticeably larger and better constructed than those in the pounds and villages. They measure 20–30 ft in internal diameter, exceptionally 30–40 ft with walls 4–5 ft thick, lined with massive granite slabs. Ex-cavation has shown that the roof of turf or thatch was supported on a centre post and a post-ring as in the pounds and a division into sleeping and working quarters was also discernible. An unu-sual structure was the large metal worker's hut at Kestor, walled off from the fields in a circular enclosure known as Round Pound. Its roof was supported on an irregular setting of posts, a single row over the working quarters, with its iron smelting furnace and forging pit, and a double row over the living-sleeping quarters where there was a subsidiary hearth. There was an opening in the roof, eccentrically placed over a shallow pit probably used by the smith for quenching, and a covered drain led from it under the wall.

At Gwithian the houses contemporary with the ploughing have not yet been located but three others which were built successively on the fields later in the Bronze Age were oval or sub-rectangular. Their construction in comparison with those on the granite was flimsy, with a slate and rubble foundation for a wall of sods. The roofs were supported on an irregular oval setting of posts, 3 to 4 ft away from the wall: two of the huts had timber porches. The hearths were circular, edged with beach pebbles and in a clay-lined hollow beside them a saddle quern, rubbing stones and part of a wooden bowl were found.

The Gwithian agricultural settlement is assigned to the early Middle Bronze Age, *c.* 1400–1200 B.C.; the incised and twisted cord (layer 5) pottery belongs to the middle group. The Smal-lacombe Rocks settlement of four huts with at least three fields near Haytor has produced rims of furrowed storage jars with

Plate 45

Fig. 25

Figs. 28, 29

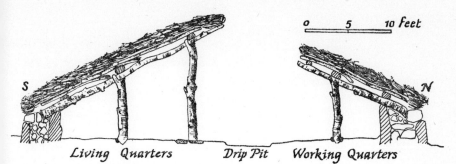

Living Quarters   Drip Pit   Working Quarters

Fig. 28. *Reconstructed section of the metal worker's hut at Kestor, Chagford, Devon*

Fig. 29. *Plan of the metal worker's hut, the Round Pound, at Kestor, Chagford, Devon*

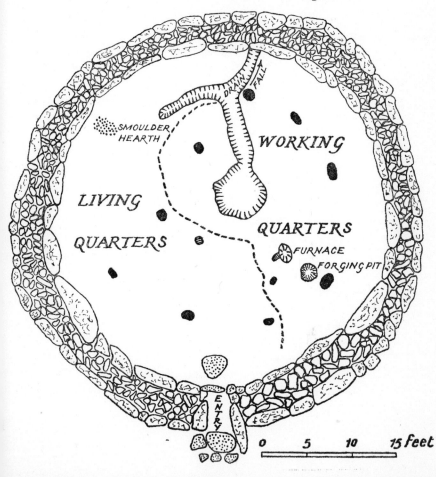

elaborate plaited cord patterns which should belong to the early group: pottery from other Dartmoor sites belongs to the middle group and is similar to that from the pastoral settle-ments. Carinated and finger-tip ornamented sherds from Foales Arrishes and Kestor show that some farms were still active in the late Bronze and early Iron Age. On Bodmin Moor also, a settlement of small huts set amongst fields on Garrow Tor, excavated by Miss D. Dudley, was occupied in the third cen-tury B.C. on the evidence of an imported La Tène I blue and yellow glass eye-bead. It is clear that once farming communities had established themselves in the uplands, their mode of life remained unaltered for a very long time.

METALLURGY, TOOLS AND WEAPONS

Many of the settlements on the granite were well-placed for the exploitation of alluvial tin and of the copper lodes, but evidence that the metals were worked is elusive. A hoard of tin nodules from a Middle Bronze Age hut at Trevisker and a droplet of slag and a cassiterite pebble from huts at Dean Moor, are the only authentic records. It can be deduced that the smelting fur-naces were situated in the mining area and not in the settlements. The surprising discovery of 50 lbs. of broken iron ore, a high-grade specular haematite, in the core of a hut wall at Dean Moor shows that the inhabitants prospected five or six miles off the granite for metals. Since the double process of smelting and forging necessary to extract workable iron was not known, the ore was regarded as waste, probably after failure to smelt it.

MIDDLE BRONZE AGE   It seems reasonable to infer that the local metals were used for the manufacture of regional types of tools and weapons. The most common tool was the palstave, an improvement on the early flanged axe by the provision of a stop-ridge between the base of the blade and the hafting hollow, and by the increased height of the flanges to grip the split 'knee' shaft. The south-

Fig. 30. Bronze palstave of south-western type from the Taunton workhouse hoard, Somerset

western form is a heavy tool, with a broadly expanding blade, often with a raised Y or V pattern below the stop-ridge, and with characteristic high flanges, which distinguish it from the low-flanged varieties of southern and eastern England. The distribution shows a concentration in the surrounds of the Somerset marshes and in Devon; a stone mould from Bigbury in the Plymouth Museum shows that it was made in south Devon. A hoard of eight found under a granite boulder at Plumley, Bovey Tracey, in 1836 must represent a metal-worker's stock, whereas the two found with the rapiers at Crediton should be the personal equipment of a chief.

The rapier too was produced locally; two sets of bi-valve stone moulds were found in the alluvial clay under 6 ft of river gravel in the metalliferous Teign valley at Knighton, Hennock. The moulds had been tied together in pairs, as though ready for casting. On the longer mould a matrix for casting a five-

Fig. 30

Fig. 31

Fig. 32

Plates 48, 49

97

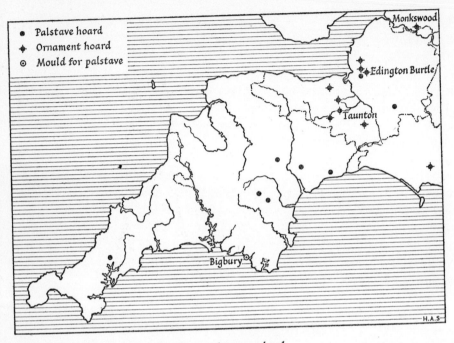

Key:
- ● Palstave hoard
- ✦ Ornament hoard
- ⊙ Mould for palstave

Fig. 31. Distribution of south-western palstave and ornament hoards

Plate 50

ribbed tapering strip has been cut, suitable for making bracelets and rings, like those in the Edington Burtle ornament hoard
in Somerset. The edges of the smaller mould have thin diagonal
vents for the escape of gases during casting: this, as Mr H. Hodges has pointed out, was a custom of the bronze-smiths of
northern Europe and was not a British or Irish practice: it suggests that the moulds at Knighton came from the workshop of
an immigrant travelling smith.

Fig. 32

Ten rapiers are known from south Devon: they include a
merchant's hoard of six at Talaton on the ridgeway between
the Otter and Clyst, two from Crediton found with the palstaves, and one from Fice's Well, Princetown, which was
sealed under 18 inches of peat. Such weapons are a reminder
that the Middle Bronze Age was not always peaceful.

There are other signs of contact between the bronze workers in the south-west and those on the continent in the Middle Bronze Age. A group of hoards in mid-Somerset, on the periphery of the marsh and in the Vale of Taunton, contain southwestern high-flanged palstaves and native spearheads with basal loops in association with knobbed sickles, torcs or necklets of twisted bronze, coiled finger-rings and bracelets of various types, all of which, as Dr Margaret Smith has shown, derive from foreign models, current in north-east and in southern Germany, *c.* 1200–1000 B.C., (Monteilius III). That these exotic things were made in Somerset is apparent in the case of the knobbed sickles, for one of those in the Edington Burtle hoard, which was found in a maple-wood chest by peat diggers, was an untrimmed casting straight from the mould.

Fig. 31

Plate 50

A rare type of slender socketed axe in the Taunton workhouse hoard which occurs in north-east Germany was copied in the south-west region on the evidence of a stone mould in the Gwithian settlement (layer 3). It affords a useful chronological and cultural link between the farmers and the smiths.

A West country connection with Iberia is indicated by the

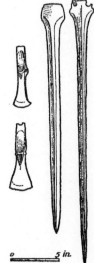

Fig. 32. The Crediton hoard of bronze rapiers and palstaves

0 _____ 5 in.

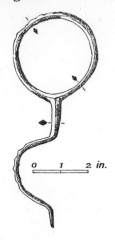

Fig. 33. Quoit pin, from the Taunton Workhouse hoard, Somerset

0   1   2 in.

palstaves with two loops, which are found in central Somerset, with outliers at Chagford, Devon, and St Mawgan-in-Menage, south Cornwall, as well as on the Dorset coast. This double-looped form was manufactured in north-west Spain and Portugal in the late Bronze Age, where moulds and untrimmed specimens are known. In Britain its association with a twisted torc and a bracelet at West Buckland near Taunton, shows that it was contemporary with the 'ornament hoards' like Edington Burtle, assigned to the end of the Middle Bronze Age.

The ornaments that are such a feature of the Somerset hoards show that a display of jewellery and elaborate dress became fashionable locally in the Middle Bronze Age, as on the continent; for instance, little bronze cones in the Monkswood hoard, near Bath, are thought to be for stitching to a skin-cloak, like one worn by a woman buried at Lübz, in east Germany. It is unfortunate that the adoption of cremation in Britain has prevented us from seeing the Middle Bronze Age chieftains and their women in their finery in the grave. The hoards show that necklets, bracelets and rings were worn and large ornamental pins with loop heads were used to fasten clothing. These 'quoit

Fig. 33

pins' as they are now called, are an insular type occurring only in the Somerset 'ornament hoards' and in Sussex: they demon-strate the inventiveness of the local metal-workers and their independence of the continental schools.

The same fashion for adornment is reflected in the contem-porary or slightly later Towednack gold hoard, which was found buried in a field bank, presumed to be Bronze Age, not far from St Ives. Here there were two splendid twisted torcs, four plain bracelets, two being unfinished, and three slender coiled bars of gold, the smith's raw material. Both torcs were made from such gold bars by heating and working them into triangu-lar form and then beating out the angles slightly into low flanges, except the terminals which were left plain and rounded; the whole was then tightly twisted clockwise, bent into form and the ends turned back as long hook fasteners. The larger torc, which is 45 inches long and was found in two coils, probably was intended for a spiral bracelet *(armilla)* of four or five coils. The smaller torc, 4½ inches across, is a technical *tour de force,* being made of three separate strands, each regularly twisted and united at the terminals. This hoard must be the stock-in-trade of a travelling Irish smith, exchanging products of his na-ve gold, made to a customer's order, for Cornish tin; it provides a glimpse of the smith in relation to local society, *c.* 900 B.C.

It is now generally agreed that there was no racial change in the last phase of the Bronze Age in the south-west. The period from 900–450 B.C. is marked only by the successive introduc-tions of new varieties of bronze tools and weapons, by an in-crease in the smith's output and in the exploitation of metals. The rapier gave way to the heavy slashing sword with a leaf-shaped blade and elongated hilt, the palstave was replaced by a variety of socketed axes and a wide range of tools, socketed knives, gouges and chisels, all ultimately of continental origin, became available for the carpenter's and metal worker's tool-kit. Nevertheless in comparison with southern and eastern

Plate 51

LATE
BRONZE AGE

Britain, the new elements are few in number and limited in kind; there are only three swords from Devon and six or seven from Cornwall, of which only one survives; in Devon, palstaves outnumber socketed axes by two to one indicating their prolonged use; founders hoards are few; none of the West Alpine novelties which are regularly associated with carp's tongue swords and winged axes in the south-east or the harness trappings which appear in the latest South Wales hoards are found in short, the peninsula became rather a backwater.

Three of the founder's hoards reveal the smiths at work. A Kenidjack Castle, St Just, some 30 pieces of copper and smelt ed tin were found in a hut outside the rampart of the Iron Ag promontory fort; with these was a broken winged axe suitabl for melting down, and two new socketed axes of south-wester type with three ribs, made of bronze with a high tin conten At Wick, Stogursey, on the north Somerset coast, a hoard 147 pieces was found in 1870. It contained several copper in gots and also bronze 'jets', the surplus metal remaining in th clay funnel when it was poured into the mould. The 17 piec of swords, a broken chape, 37 damaged axes and spearhead and a couple of palstaves were material collected for the meltir pot, whilst the socketed axes, gouges and knives were ne products ready for sale.

Two types of looped and socketed axes were made in t south-west. The first is a heavy tool with three converging divergent ribs and with a broad flat-topped moulding rour the socket. Two sets of stone moulds for these came from He bury, near Camelford: they are unusual in having a guide li on the ends for keying the moulds together instead of dov holes, and in the matrix being cut flush with the top of t mould, instead of providing a hollow for the insertion of clay core and pouring 'gate'. The distribution of such axes practically confined to the south-west and to South Wal since the majority have been found in Glamorgan, it is of

Plate 52b

Plates 52a, c

called the Welsh axe, though no worshop has been found there. From its association in hoards on both sides of the Bristol Channel, for instance at Kenidjack with a discarded winged axe, and at Llynfawr with cauldrons, harness trappings and an iron Hallstatt sword, it was manufactured towards the end of the Bronze Age, probably in the sixth century B.C.

The second socketed axe mould was found on the Quantocks and is of bronze which was more usually employed than stone at this time. It is said that such bi-valve moulds were used by the smiths for the quick production of bees' wax models for casting by the *cire-perdue* process; but as Mr Hodges has pointed out in a recent study, the cutting of two recesses at the mouth of the Quantock mould is a device to prevent a clay socket core riding up during casting, so it can be presumed that they were employed for direct casting. No axes from the mould have been found so it is evidently the work of an isolated local smith.

Although the south-west lay outside the main stream of continental connections in the late Bronze Age, trading contacts with Brittany and with Ireland were maintained. From Brittany came characteristic straight-sided square-socketed axes, of which 40 or 50 were found at Higher Roseworthy, Gwinnear in 1880, and others on Carn Brea, near Redruth. Two were found in a tin stream under 12 ft of black mud at Lanherne, St Mawgan-in-Pyder, together with other socketed axes, a saw, a Middle Bronze Age rapier and palstave. These Breton axes are curious in that many of them are non-functional, being badly made of thin metal, often with a high proportion of lead and with the casting seams left on and the blade unsharpened. They are found in great quantities in the Breton hoards and it is probable that they were used as a primitive currency both in their homeland and for export. It is difficult to suggest what brought their merchants to the south-west, since Brittany possesses both tin and copper of her own and they had no need to cross the Channel for it.

The Irish finds are more spectacular: they include a hoard of six gold bracelets from Morvah in the Land's End peninsula, three with attractive hollow trumpet-mouth ends, two with solid expanded terminals and one with folded-back ends: the type with expanded terminals occurs in the well-known Beachy Head hoard with a carp's tongue sword and a winged axe and is of seventh century date. Two large bronze vessels found in 1792 by tin miners working on Broadwater Moor, Luxulyan, near St Austell, but unfortunately not preserved, are likely to be of Irish manufacture and late Bronze Age date: one was said to be a conical vessel hammered out of a single sheet of bronze, perhaps a bucket, the other was a cauldron made of strips of bronze riveted together and had elaborate attachments for the handles on the rim; similar cauldrons were exported from Ireland in the seventh and sixth centuries to Wales, southern Britain and the Atlantic coasts, so this Cornish find falls into place on a recognised trade route.

Towards the end of the Bronze Age, the climate deteriorated as the warm wet sub-Atlantic phase set in, producing a growth of peat on the high moors and culminating *circa* 500–400 B.C. in an inundation in the Somerset levels, which became a sedge fen. The onset was gradual from *circa* 900 B.C.: to overcome it, Late Bronze Age peoples living on the perimeter and islanded on the Polden ridge built timber trackways and platforms on the surface of the raised bogs. The trackway across Meare Heath which has been traced for $1\frac{1}{2}$ miles, consisted of a corduroy of heavy oak and birch timbers on a brushwood foundation and held in place by stakes driven through square mortise holes: the stakes also retained a kerb of longitudinal timbers, presumably for the benefit of wheeled traffic. Radiocarbon analysis has dated timber in this trackway to *circa* 880 B.C. ($\pm$ 110), but other tracks on Shapwick Heath belong to the 6th century. They reflect the vain struggle to maintain communications against the rising flood waters.

Ve turn now to the burial rites of the Bronze Age people as
vealed by the numerous barrows raised to their dead. A con-
rvative reckoning based on the Ordnance Survey maps shows
out 875 surviving in Cornwall, 550 in Devon. They are
und not only on the granite moors but on some of the Culm
ay ridges in mid and west Devon, around Halwill, Hols-
orthy, and in the Hartland peninsula. Their distribution re-
cts the well-known improvement in the sub-Boreal climate,
hich permitted the colonisation of heavier soil. The distribu-
n on the moors is apparently unrelated to the settlements: for
stance, in the Avon valley, south Dartmoor, there are 33
tlements containing over 200 huts and only 8 barrows on the
rrounding hills. Obviously the graves of the majority of the
pulation were not permanently marked and not even that
every chieftain.

The site chosen was usually a summit from which the mound
conspicuous over a wide tract of country, as for example
ree Barrows at 1550 ft above the Erme on Dartmoor, or
apman barrows at 1575 ft on Exmoor: others were erected
ntervals along the ridgeways as on the Brendon Hills whilst
the plateaux and lower ground the barrow is often placed
a 'false crest', and is conspicuous from one approach. The
d were thus set apart from the likely settlement zone, the
er ground by the springheads, but interred in places where
y were brought to mind as men and women moved about
hills with the herds.

he grouping of the mounds implies that individual com-
nities had their own burial grounds, well exemplified on
noor in the clusters of barrows along the 1500 ft ridge be-
en the Barle and Bray on the present Devon-Somerset
ndary. In such cemeteries, the cairns are irregularly spaced
n the Five Barrows (actually eight); only exceptionally are
aligned as the seven out of the eleven in the Chapman

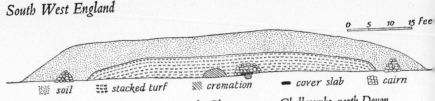

0   5   10   15 Fee

:::: soil   ::::: stacked turf   \\\\\ cremation   ━ cover slab   ▦ cairn

Fig. 34. Reconstructed section of a barrow in the Chapman group, Challacombe, north Devon

group. In other districts, the barrows may be dispersed ov
more than a mile of plateau as at Halwill, or on the Taphou
ridge east of Lostwithiel, leaving the surrounding area blan

Plate 53
BURIAL RITES

It is now axiomatic that a barrow is not just a heap of ear
or stones covering a burial, but the result of a series of ritual ac
and constructions by a community, which it is the task of
excavator to elucidate by slow and careful work. The rou;
and ready methods of the eighteenth and nineteenth centu
antiquaries and their inadequate records do not provide t
material for this sort of interpretation, and since very few scie
tific excavations have taken place in this region, our knowled
is limited.

Single cremation burials were the normal method of dispo
of the dead. The ashes were collected from the pyre and broug
to the chosen site and buried, often in an urn, which was son
times placed in a pit, but more frequently in a small cist bel
ground level and covered by a flat slab. The place was th
usually marked by a small cairn or mound before the full-s

Fig. 34

barrow was built, as for instance at Chapman Barrows on I
moor. Such monuments, in effect, are a tribute to the individ
reflecting presumably his or her importance in the commun
the concept originated with the Beaker folk and is eviden
the inhumations of the early Bronze Age (p. 70): on
evidence of the urns, it continued to dominate fun
practice throughout the Middle Bronze Age.

Secondly, there are multiple interments, as for example,
four cremations in urns, one in a cist, one inverted on a
slab and another erect, found under a round cairn at Cla

Gardens, Mullion. Others described by W.C.Borlase are Carn Creis with five urns, one ribbon-handled and one with faience beads, Carn Lesky with seven urns and Trannack, Madron, with five or six urns. The surviving urns from these barrows vary in style and form but there is not enough evidence to decide whether such burying places were used for some time as a flat cemetery before being covered by the cairn or barrow, or whether the burials were simultaneous. A flat cemetery with urns in style 1 and 2 has been found at Port Mellon, Meva-gissey. In these interments the megalithic idea of communal burial is in evidence and it is not surprising that all known examples are in Cornwall. The Entrance Graves (p. 51) which contain a succession of cremations, some like Knackyboy in similar Middle Bronze Age urns, are another expression of the same idea.

Plate 39

Thirdly there are ritual barrows, in which the primary de-posit consists of charcoal or other substances in a central pit or beneath a small cairn. The human remains, whether one or several, are buried usually in urns some distance away, in a manner aptly termed by Ashbee as 'satellite burial'. The im-plication is that a ritual act, which probably was believed to establish contact with the underworld, preceeded the burial and was of prime importance. An elaborate example of a ritual barrow has been recently excavated by Mrs P.Christie at Crig-a-Mennis, near Perranzabuloe: here a low central cairn covered only a deposit of oak charcoal spread on the old ground surface and filling a small hole: two fine ribbon-handled urns (style 1) and a miniature cup were buried in pits 15 to 20 ft away in different directions within a ditched enclosure and a cairn-ring. Since neither urn contained human remains, it was concluded that the whole monument was a cenotaph. The Hameldon dagger burial previously described (p. 75) is a dated instance of a satellite to a small cairn covering only char-coal. At Brownstone Farm, Kingswear, a cremation with a

Fig 35

Plates 54, 55

Fig. 19

miniature polished axe in a stone cist was placed 8 feet away from the centre of the mound at which there was a small hole tight-packed with the burnt bones of a child of ten; the primary ritual act implied here is a sacrifice. At Combe Beacon, St Nicholas, Somerset, there was no burial; the large turf barrow, 10 ft high, with a central cairn of chert covered only a small hole domed over with loamy soil and filled with oak, ash and hazel charcoal. These customs originate in the early Bronze Age (Wessex phase) in our area, and are widely distributed; similar rites are known in south Wales in the middle or late Bronze Age.

CONSTRUC-
TION

Fig. 34
Fig. 35

Plate 40

The mound covering any of these three varieties of burial was built either of stones, turf, or earth, or was composite, containing separate deposits of each. Often small stones were used to build a cairn-ring; at Hameldon this marked the edge of the mound, at Chapman Barrow it encircled a turf stack but was covered by soil, whilst at Crig-a-Mennis only a segment was built which was covered by the mound. At Elworthy, Somerset, a circle of upright stones about 6 ft in diameter and 3 ft high surrounded a cremation in an urn with incised decoration (style 2) and was concealed in the body of the mound. Revetments of large blocks either laid horizontally (a kerb) or set upright (a peristalith) were frequently built at the circumference of cairns on Dartmoor (the so-called retaining circle), on Exmoor as at Setta Barrow, and in Cornwall: these were functional, they retained the soil and enhanced the final appearance; the concealed features, on the other hand, were magical, designed to protect the ashes of the dead from molestation, and to confine the spirits to their tomb.

Two conclusions emerge from the records of barrows opened in this region: first, there was no uniformity in burial practice or barrow construction, even in one district, or among examples that have produced the same sort of pottery. Each community must have built up its own tradition, new elements

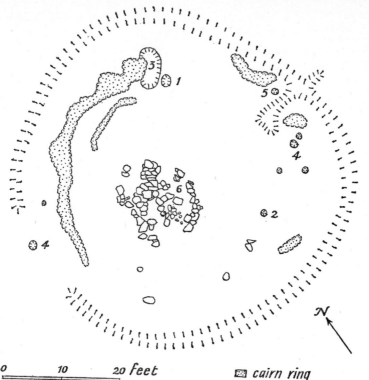

Fig. 35. Plan of Crig-a-Mennis barrow, Perranzabuloe, Cornwall. 1-2. urn pits; 3-4. ritual pits; 5. miniature cup; 6. stone area

perhaps being acquired through marriage. Secondly, whilst Bronze Age funeral practice embodies several elements with a Beaker or Megalithic ancestry, the elaboration of barrow build-ing is associated with the earlier forms of ribbon-handled urns (style 1) or with Wessex grave-goods, on present dating to *circa* 1400 B.C. Apparently no new rites or structural innovations were introduced after the beginning of the Middle Bronze Age and whilst barrow building still continued to be extensively practised, the traditions were in decay. There are very few barrows containing pottery that can be assigned to the late Bronze Age with any certainty at present, though there are many on record which contained plain cremations which may belong to this epoch. On the other hand, it is possible that after 900 B.C. the custom of barrow-making died out in the south-west, and everyone was buried in flat cemeteries, which as yet have eluded the archaeologist.

CHAPTER VII

The Celtic Peoples

DURING THE IRON AGE immigration began again from the continent; groups of Celtic peoples crossed from northern and western France and Belgium to settle in strength in southern Britain. They came in three waves, the first during the fifth and fourth centuries B.C. with pottery and equipment of late Hallstatt type that had been developed on the continent during the previous 200 years; their culture is known as Iron A, and is poorly represented in the south-west. The second wave, the B groups, brought a fully developed La Tène I culture, characterised by decorated metalwork and pottery; they effected first local infiltrations, which were followed by a massive and widespread intrusion in the south-west in the third and second centuries B.C. The last wave, the C groups, came to Britain from the late second till the mid first centuries B.C. in consequence of the invasions of Gaul by Germanic tribes, the Cimbri and Teutons, in 120–110 B.C. and by Julius Caesar in 58–50 B.C.: the Belgic tribes of south-eastern and southern England were the principal intruders but other small refugee groups can be distinguished in the south-west. At the end of the Iron Age, an amalgam of these three groups in the peninsula, together with Bronze Age survivors on the high moorland, were known as the Dumnonii, and were so named by the Greek geographer, Ptolemy, when he compiled his map at Alexandria in the second century A.D.

Celtic society differed in many respects from the preceding Bronze Age civilisation. The population was politically more unified and organised in larger units, in tribes under chieftains and in tribal confederacies under kings. Women also played an important part in the social order judging by the rich possessions buried in their graves. The struggles between the tribes

for land and wealth made the Celts an alert, adventurous ar
bellicose people. Warfare now was a major preoccupatio
shown both in the labour diverted to building elaborate forti
cations and in the craftsmanship devoted to the panoply of th
warrior-chiefs. Under the aegis of the Dumnonii the trade i
Cornish tin flourished, with Gallic merchants acting as middl
men for the Mediterranean market; Diodorus Siculus recor
that they found the inhabitants peacable and friendly to strai
gers. Agriculture however was the mainstay of the econom
and as we shall see in the hill-forts, stock-keeping rather tha
corn-growing was predominant.

THE FIRST PHASE

SETTLEMENTS
AND BURIALS The first Celtic peoples differed little in their way of life fro
the Bronze Age agriculturalists (p. 92): they too lived peasan
fashion in open settlements in round huts and cultivated sma
fields as at Bodrifty on the granite near Penzance or at Dainto
on the Devonian limestone near Newton Abbot. The mai
difference lies in the pottery they used, which includes charac
teristic small bowls and tall necked pots with a carination an
splayed rim common to the Iron A peoples in southern Britai
At Dainton a ferruginous slip was used to redden the surfac
of some vessels in imitation of the haematite wares of Wesse
whilst at Bodrifty some fine wares were burnished. Some Bronz
Age sherds at Bodrifty indicate that the two peoples mingle
whilst on Dartmoor the few Iron Age sherds from huts
Kestor and Foales Arrishes suggest that the newcomers we
absorbed by the native population in the upland.

They brought, however, to this region the knowledge of iro
working which had eluded the metalworkers at Dean Moo
(p. 96). The process differs from that of tin and copper smel
ing in that the metal has to be extracted from the ore in tw
stages: the first smelt produces only a spongy bloom that is fu

of impurities; it has then to be reheated, hammered on an anvil and quenched to purify, toughen and consolidate the metal. In the metalworker's hut at Kestor the dual process was in evi-dence; there was a small bowl furnace full of iron slag, the residue from the last smelt, a forging-pit burnt red, a quenching place with a drain and an anvil stone. The ore used was a specular haematite from the Hennock district ten miles away. The new metal thus produced was malleable; tools and wea-pons no longer had to be cast and were easier to produce and to repair. Communities were no longer dependent on the itinerant merchant-smith for their everyday needs, which was a real advance.

Figs. 28, 29

The Celtic peoples re-introduced inhumation burial: at the large cemetery found beneath 15 ft of sand-dune in 1900–05 at Harlyn Bay, Padstow, the dead were buried in a contracted position in rectangular coffins of thin slate slabs. Grave-goods included a bronze swan-neck pin and two iron-ring headed pins, two La Tène I brooches of a type found in north-west Spain, earrings and a bracelet, all of which date from the late fourth and third century B.C. The same rite of cist burial with the corpse contracted and adorned for burial persisted throughout the Iron Age and into the Roman period. It can be seen in cemeteries at Mount Batten, Plymouth and Trelan Bahow, St Keverne, where noble women wearing bracelets, beads and La Tène III brooches were interred with their decorated mir-rors or with imported glass vessels early in the first century A.D. and at Porth Cressa and Poynter's Garden in the Scilly Islands in the first and second centuries A.D. At Harlyn Bay there was a midden beside the cemetery, indicating there was a settlement at this sheltered site. The occupants made needles, awls and borers for leather from the local slate as well as loomweights and spindle whorls for their weaving and spinning. They also used bone weaving-combs and bobbins whilst a quantity of *Purpurea lapillus* shells, from which purple dyes are extracted,

Plate 56

Plate 76

Plate 57

Plate 56

shows that they may have produced coloured cloth. The brooches of an Iberian pattern in the cemetery suggest that there
were visiting traders to the bay, if not immigrants, from the
Atlantic coasts in the fourth or third centuries B.C. Decorated
pottery from the midden shows that the occupation continued
into the second and first centuries B.C.

At Mount Batten, the promontory on the eastern side of
Plymouth Sound, an important trading settlement was established also at this time, taking advantage of the sheltered anchorage and of easy routes to western Dartmoor and to the
metalliferous regions south-east of Bodmin Moor. Pottery from
a midden on the shore shows that the site was occupied throughout the Iron Age, starting with tall situlate jars of late southern
A type with which a swan-neck pin and another example of
an Iberian La Tène I brooch can be associated. There were
also several ribbed and knobbed bronze bracelets of late Hallstatt or early La Tène continental patterns, for which the nearest
source would be Normandy or Brittany, and which indicate
cross-channel trading contacts.

FORTIFICA-
TIONS

The beginnings of fortification show that some intrusive
groups became uneasy in their new lands, probably when
further invasions threatened at the close of the third century B.C.
Blackbury Castle started about this time as a single ramparted
fort of four acres, on the narrow back of a greensand spur in
east Devon. The pottery used has affinities with that produced
by late southern Iron A peoples at Maiden Castle in Dorset,
and indicates the origin of the settlers. The gateway to the fort
was strongly fortified by building up the out-turned ends of the
rampart with layers of chert and flint nodules which were held
in place by a timber palisade; in effect the door was flanked
by low semi-circular towers or fighting platforms, which were
connected by a timber bridge set back over the gate. An unusual barbican outwork was added later making the fort a
multiple-enclosure type.

At Maen Castle, on the wind-swept granite cliffs above Sennen Cove, Land's End, a small promontory was fortified by another early group, using plain undecorated pottery in the 'A' tradition. The defences were a thick wall of granite blocks packed in soil, with a berm separating it from the ditch, and a counter-scarp bank. There was a single entrance, facing east towards a zone of small terraced fields. Since no permanent dwellings were found in the fort, the builders presumably lived in a more sheltered spot beyond the cultivation.

It is only because these two forts have been carefully excavated that we are able to assign them to the first phase of Iron Age settlement: there are many univallate forts and cliff castles such as Cadson Bury near Callington or Golden at Probus, that may prove to have originated at this time.

It is apparent that from the sixth century B.C. there were trading contacts between south-west Britain and the Armorican peninsula. The late Latin poem *Ora Maritima* of Avienus incorporates fragments of a very early topographical account of the north-western coasts, known as the Massiliote Periplus, by a Greek voyager. From this, it is learnt that Tartessians from southern Spain and Carthaginians voyaged as far as Brittany (*Oestrymnis*) and its offshore islands to trade: thence the natives sailed in skin boats to Ireland which is called Ierne and to Britain which is called Albion.

OVERSEAS TRADE

Early in the fifth century the Carthaginians conquered Tartessos and gained control of the rich mineral deposits in southern Spain which had supplied the Greek city states in the Mediterranean; thus a fresh demand arose for tin from north-west Europe. This is the economic background to the voyage of Pytheas, a Greek merchant and geographer, who in 330–325 B.C. sailed up the Atlantic coasts to Britain and the far north. His account unfortunately has not survived except in quotation by later writers; his experiences, for instance, are referred to by Strabo in his *Geography* but only usually to disparage them.

By the second century B.C. it is clear from the *History* of Diodorus Siculus that regular trade routes from the Mediterranean
to Britain were established, a thirty days march overland from
the Rhône to the Garonne via the Carcassone gap, thence by
sea to Corbilo (Nantes) on the Loire, and on in fair weather
to round the Armorican peninsula and a four days voyage
'across Ocean' to south-west Britain. Gallic merchants were
the intermediaries, principally the Veneti from southern Brittany
until the savage destruction of their fleet by Caesar in 56 B.C.

Archaeological confirmation of direct contact with the Mediterranean is slender and frequently suspect, but continues to
accumulate. Beside four Greek *lekythoi* of the fifth century from
Halamanning, St Hiliary, in Penwith, there are a pair of two-
handled Attic cups *(borsae)* and a jug *(oinochoe)* in the Torquay
Museum from 'an artificial cave at Teignmouth' which are
assigned to the fourth century B.C. At Holne above the Dart
near Buckfast a worn silver coin of Alexander the Great and
another of Aesillas the Roman quaestor in Macedonia in 90
B.C. were found separately by a ploughman and seem genuine
imports. In Exeter, apart from a mixed collection of Mediterranean coins found in Broadgate in 1810–20 which remain
suspect, copper coins of the cities of Velia and Paestum in
south Italy were found in 1931, though unstratified; others were
recorded by a reliable antiquary, Captain W.P.Shortt in the
1830's and 40's. Recently a hoard of 43 silver drachmae has
been recovered from Paul, near Penzance, minted by Celtic
tribes in Cisalpine Gaul and modelled on those of Massilia:
their date lies in the late second century B.C.

There is thus a growing body of evidence that can not be
disregarded. Not all these tokens were necessarily exchanged
for tin. Diodorus also states that in Gaul merchants would give
a jar of wine for a slave (V. 26). The great H-shaped tin ingot
weighing 158 lbs and 'shaped like an *astragalus*' as Diodorus
described, which was dredged up near St Mawes, Falmouth,

Plates 58, 59

Plate 60

116

must be but one of many that were brought down by pack-horses or wagons to be loaded into the ships of the Veneti, an-chored in the deep estuary or off St Michael's Mount *(Ictis).*

THE SECOND PHASE

The effective Celtic settlement of the peninsula took place in the late third and second centuries B.C. by peoples from north-western France who had been in contact with the advanced La Tène civilisations of the Marne; they introduced new varie-ties of pottery and metal work and developed a regional style of fortification suited to a pastoral economy. Their culture is termed South-Western Third B in Professor Hawkes' classi-fication: the movements of earlier groups (First B) to the south and east of England, and the resulting fusion with the A peoples there (Second B cultures) are not really represented in the south-west which pursued an independent course.

IRON AGE B
IMMIGRANTS

The new decorated ceramic, which is the hall-mark of South-Western Third B is a dark smooth ware, sometimes worked over with wet hands to produce the appearance of a slip: the bowls and jars are rounded with a well-marked neck and everted rim, sometimes finished on a turn-table or slow wheel. The decoration is boldly incised on the shoulder, using a 'blunt point'. The patterns which also occur on metal-work are composed of scrolls and curves, often emphasised by surface moulding, particularly by a depression at the head of a scroll, whilst other elements are brought out by an infilling of diagonal or cross-hatching: in the best examples there is a subtle inter-play between the plain and hatched surfaces. An internal groove on the lip of both plain and decorated pots is also a characteristic innovation.

POTTERY

Plates 61, 64

The decorated pottery is distributed generally in the penin-sula apart from the high moorlands and north Devon. There is an important concentration in Somerset, centred in the lake

Fig. 36

Plates 62, 63

villages of Meare and Glastonbury where it was first discovered by Bulleid and Gray and named 'Glastonbury ware'. The Somerset pottery is, however, more sophisticated; the potters use a finer point for the incisions and have a larger répertoire of designs, including motifs like the triquetra, the swastika, fret or the returning spiral. The explanation seems to be that the Somerset colonists were in an area where there was a flourishing school of metalwork with a tradition going back to Bronze Age times, whereas in Devon and Cornwall the metalworkers were concerned with mining and were without a sustained interest in design.

The origin of the B pottery and the people who made it is still obscure though Brittany remains the most likely source. In general, Breton La Tène pottery of the third and second cen׳ turies is different but there are a few pieces like the decorated jars from St׳Pol׳de׳Lèon and Plouhinec which have long been held to be ancestral to the British series. These have incised disigns with a stippled infilling, which are transcripts of those on Marnian metal׳work of the fourth century; some simple patterns like the scallop or broken arcading occur both in Somerset and in the Morbihan. The pots with internal׳grooved rims are also a type which is localised in north׳western France and south׳western England as Sir Mortimer Wheeler has shown. However it is clear that decorated pottery took root in south׳west Britain, and in company with the metal׳work, de׳ veloped a regional style which is not found on the continent.

Other immigrants from the Atlantic coasts are indicated by another sort of pottery with stamped decoration, Z or S shaped impressions that are the vestiges of a row of stylised ducks. Analogies are found in the *castros* of north׳west Spain and Portugal, the same region from which the La Tène I brooches were derived (p. 114) and also sporadically in Brittany. The British distribution shows that the immigrants sailed up the Bristol Channel to settle in the lower Severn and Wye valleys;

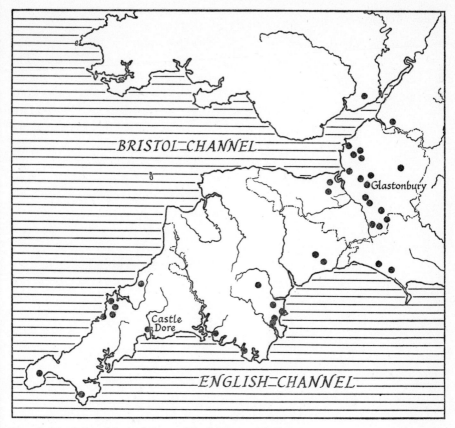

Fig. 36. Distribution of decorated pottery of South-Western Third B type

their culture is known as Western Third B. Some stamped sherds have been found at Chun, an unusual circular walled fort in the Land's End peninsula, at Gurnards Head cliff-castle and at a few other coastal sites in Cornwall. At St Mawgan-in-Pyder, Newquay (p. 128), some were associated with curvilinear incised wares in the huts of a fortified settlement first occupied in the late first century B.C. The evidence is not yet sufficient to determine whether a small-scale intrusion into Cornwall

119

took place as part of a primary movement to Britain in the late third or early second century or whether it was effected later, when colonies were established in the Severn region.

HILL FORTS   The numerous settlements of the 'B' immigrants were nearly all fortified: they vary in size, scale and layout from that appro-priate to a small homestead to that of a large tribal *oppidum*. They are built not only on sites with good natural defences, but also on hill-slopes and on plateau sites. Their builders did not, how-

Fig. 37   ever, penetrate beyond the fringes of Dartmoor and Bodmin Moor, leaving the upland to the Bronze Age hut-dwellers.

Very few hill-forts have been excavated and their classifica-tion and interpretation is based mainly on surface inspection. We can distinguish three categories (i) Large forts with single or multiple close-set ramparts, (ii) Forts with several enclosures, formed by wide-spaced ramparts, (iii) Small forts with single ramparts, promontory forts and cliff-castles being included in these groups.

(i) These large forts *(oppida)* are all defensively sited, occu-pying the crest of hills or the end of a spur, as Dumpdon and Hembury forts near Honiton, or a seaward promontory as at

Plates 65, 66   Trevelegue. The size ranges between 3 and 15 acres; among
Plates 67, 68   the largest are Carnyke where a single earth rampart and ditch is aligned along the contour of an isolated hill near Bodmin, and Countisbury near Lynmouth where the top of a steep spur between the sea and East Lyn river is defended by a massive bank and ditch across the neck. In the multivallate forts, the inner rampart dominated the defences: the succession of close-set ditches and outer banks were built as obstacles to be crossed when the attackers came into range of sling-stones and other missiles. The ramparts usually were of *glacis* construction, the upcast from the ditch being formed into a continuous slope so as to create a long steep incline which gave no foothold for an assault. The builders took every advantage of the natural slopes:

Plate 66   this is well seen at Hembury where the ramparts along the steep

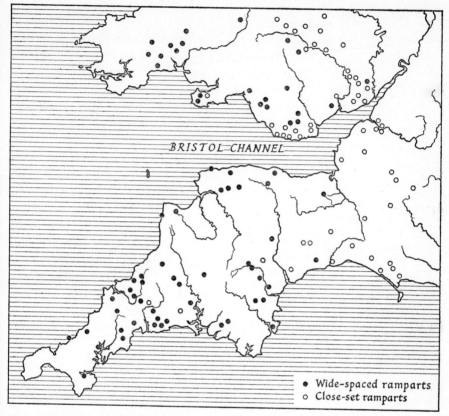

● Wide-spaced ramparts
○ Close-set ramparts

Fig. 37. Distribution of multivallate hill-forts

sides of the spur have been made by scarping and by throwing
the soil from the ditches downhill: in contrast the level ap⁄
proach across the neck was fortified by three massive ramparts
thrown up from the ditches, one being unfinished, with arti⁄
ficial inclines that measure 50–55 ft long. In other forts such as
Sidbury, east Devon, the size of the ramparts is also nicely
adjusted to the risk of attack.

The entrances in this class of fort were ingeniously construct⁄
ed, and obviously were the focus of attack. At Hembury west
entrance, the approach up the hillside was made into a bottle⁄

neck by linking the ends of the ramparts with a bank screening the ditch ends and revetting it with large timbers. The assailants would have to fight their way up this narrow passage before they reached the double gate, which was probably surmounted by a timber bridge to enable the defenders to pass from one side to the other. Attackers were also enfiladed by out-turning the rampart ends as at Musbury and Sidbury forts in east Devon.

Fig. 37

The large multivallate forts are found, with few exceptions, to east of the Exe. Their designs are closely linked with the forts of the Durotriges, the tribes in Dorset and south Somerset. Nevertheless Hembury was built by peoples using South-Western B decorated pottery, whom we may now call the Dumnonii.

The multivallate cliff-castles on the north coast of Cornwall must be the work of another overseas group entering the Bristol Channel. The great fort on Trevelgue Head, Newquay, with four close-set ramparts defending the narrowest part of the promontory, an inner enclosure and an outer annexe is obviously a work of several periods but since the excavations of 1939 are unpublished, its origin remains an enigma. Similar massing of ramparts can be seen in promontory forts in south Wales as at Castle Ditches, Llantwit Major, and is also a feature of the first fort at Worlebury, Weston-super-Mare, which has four lines of defence across a limestone spur. The triple rampart fort on Gurnard's Head is structurally related to a Breton fort, Ker-caradec, near Quimper: excavation has shown that both have a massive inner stone rampart, with a vertical face and stepped back, providing a stance for slingers. The same feature has been found at two promontory forts in County Cork, Portadoona and Carrigillihy, which suggests another colonising movement by Veneti up the western seaways in the second century B.C.

Plates 67, 68

It should be added that there are a few large forts on the granite that have dry-stone ramparts, like Trencrom, a fine contour fort near St Ives or the Cheesewring on Bodmin Moor,

at which rocky outcrops were skilfully incorporated in the circuit. The Dewerstone promontory fort on the western fringe
of Dartmoor was defended by two dry-walls, whilst Chun,
Land's End (p. 119) has a massive inner wall and an outer rampart. It is not yet clear whether this use of stone is of cultural
significance, indicating some fresh immigrants, widely dispersed but with a common building tradition, or whether it is
due to using what is easiest and customary on the granite.

(ii) The multiple-enclosure forts are numerous and widespread west of the Exe and have good claims to be a regional   *Fig. 37*
type, although they are also found in south Wales and occasionally in southern England. Some of them are defensively sited,
like Prestonbury in the Teign gorge but many are hidden away   Plate 70
on hill-slopes, and on wooded spurs overlooked by higher
ground and so at a tactical disadvantage if attacked. These forts
consist of a circular or sub-rectangular inner enclosure of $\frac{1}{2}$ to 4
acres, with one or more larger outer enclosures, either concentric
with it as at Clovelly Dykes, or dependent from it as at Castle   Plate 71
Dore, or annexed to it as at Helsbury. A favourite site is the end   Plate 69
of a spur where the outer enclosure could be defended by a
crossbank as at Hall Rings, Pelynt. Some cliff-castles also have   *Fig. 38*
wide-spaced ramparts, for instance Embury Beacon in the Hartland peninsula.

The ramparts are small-scale, and in contrast to the multivallate *oppida*, the outermost is usually the largest, as at the
concentric fort Tregear Rounds, St Kew. The entrances are
simple; sometimes the rampart ends were knobbed or thickened
as at Clovelly, rarely inturned as at Prestonbury or screened as
at Pencarrow. The line of approach through the enclosures was
sometimes embanked as at Wooston or Resugga and often   Plate 72
deeply worn, indicating the regular passage of stock. Frequently
the entrances are orientated towards springs and the outer ramparts are aligned to control them, showing the importance of a
water-supply.

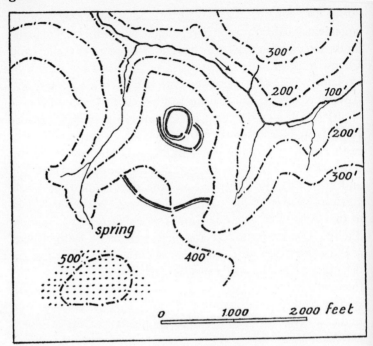

Fig. 38. Plan of Hall Rings, hill-slope fort, Pelynt, Cornwall

The layout of these forts provided a defended dwelling place for a chieftain and his kin in the innermost enclosure, with accomodation for stock in the outer enclosures, secure against cattle raiders. At Clovelly Dykes, there are four zones of out-works with restricted entry, suggesting segregation of the herds for milking, or for autumn slaughter.

Excavation at Castle Dore and Milber has shown that the inhabitants were using decorated B pottery from the begin-ning: imported La Tène glass bracelets and beads at Castle Dore show that this fort was in being by 200–150 B.C., whilst Milber near Newton Abbot, was built about 100 B.C. and went

Plate 71

Plate 61

out of use *circa* A.D. 25. Several forts have surface signs of en-
largement or re-fortification, which indicate a long life. Analogies
for the fort plans can be found in some of the *castros* of Galicia and
Orense in north-west Spain but their peculiarities can also be
explained as insular developments, due to the adoption of a
pastoral economy suited to the south-western environment.

(iii) Small forts defended by a single rampart are known as
Rounds in Cornwall: they are numerous in mid and north-
east Cornwall, and also occur in mid and north-west Devon.
They are generally situated on undulating ground between 200
and 400 ft and in Cornwall on land that is good for arable
cultivation. Most of them are circular or oval enclosures of half
to two acres with a simple entrance by a causeway across the
ditch; a few are rectilinear and may well be of Roman date.

Excavation at Castle Gotha, St Austell, has shown that the
defences of this one and a half acre enclosure were erected before 100 B.C. and that the occupation continued well into the
second century A.D. The inhabitants lived in timber huts built
in the lee of the ramparts; they included metalworkers who used
clay-lined pits, hearths and a stone mould for casting penna-
nular bracelets. An ingot mould was also found embedded in
the latest floor in one hut, probably for tin from the nearby
Pentuan streams. At Trevisker Round, St Eval, only two large
huts were built in the oval two acre enclosure, which superseded
the Bronze Age open settlement (p. 85). Iron Age pottery
used at both sites included plain and decorated South-Western
B wares.

The Rounds are thus more like a defended hamlet or homestead built by a kin-group rather than a hill-fort built by a tribe;
in scale and character they are not unlike the enclosed Bronze
Age settlements on the granite moors (p. 86). In Ireland the
type is known as a rath or ring-fort, and had a long life, continuing through the Dark Ages and early Christian period,

and it would not be surprising if some Cornish examples were inhabited also in post-Roman times.

OPEN
SETTLEMENTS
Other settlements of the 'B' people are the undefended hamlets and farmsteads in which the occupants lived in stone or timber huts, as for example at Kynance Gate, Lizard. At Bodrifty, the huts of the 'A' settlers were rebuilt in better granite masonry and 3 acres of surrounding farmland enclosed by a stone wall at this time. In West Penwith other hut groups were started in the middle Iron age that continued as 'courtyard-house' villages in the Roman period, such as Goldherring or Porthmeor, to be described in the next chapter.

The famous lake villages of Meare and Glastonbury can be regarded as flourishing outposts of the south-western B culture. They were founded *circa* 150 B.C. presumably by Dumnonian colonists coming up the Bristol Channel and penetrating by the river Brue, who imposed themselves on the local 'A' inhabitants. The decorated pottery distribution indicates their spread inland to the Mendips and to Clevedon.

Fig. 36

The marsh settlements were built on artificial islands or crannogs formed from a mass of logs, brushwood, clay and rubble systematically laid down on the edge of open water, the former Meare pool. At Glastonbury a wicker-work stockade secured to uprights driven into the peat was constructed on the perimeter and also a causeway leading out to a deep water anchorage. On these foundations, a tight-packed agglomeration of timber huts was built, 89 on the two acre site at Glastonbury, about 60 in each of the two crannogs at Meare. The huts were round, 18–28 ft in diameter, with floors and hearths of clay which needed frequent renewals due to the compacting and subsidence of the underlying strata.

The numerous finds recovered from the prolonged and painstaking excavations by H. St. George Gray and A. H. Bulleid from 1892 onwards are witness to a diversity of local crafts and industries, and to a prosperity far greater than any as yet found farther west. There were furnaces and crucibles of metal-workers in bronze and enamel, a wide range of iron tools, small objects made of Mendip lead, many bone weaving-combs and whorls indicating a domestic textile industry, decorated wooden tubs and bowls, products of skilled turners and carpenters, as well as the decorated pottery previously described (p. 118). Some cordoned wares of the Late Iron Age indicate that the villages were inhabited into the first century A.D. Plates 62, 63

These creative centres were linked by trade with Cornwall as shown by the sceptre-like tin ingot from Glastonbury, with the iron-producing centres of the Forest of Dean as shown by currency-bars, and with the Durotriges of south Dorset as shown by small objects of Kimmeridge shale. It is likely that fine bronzes made in the villages or in workshops in north Somerset which is rich in Celtic metalwork, were traded back in return; the bowls from Youlton, Cornwall, Rose Ash, north Devon, and Birdlip, Glos. are examples. Clear glass beads with attractive inlaid patterns of chrome yellow threads which were plentiful at Meare were other trade goods, reaching as far afield as Pen Dinas hill-fort, Aberystwyth, and northern Ireland. Plates 81–84

Plate 73

THE THIRD PHASE

Towards the end of the Iron Age two more groups of Celtic peoples penetrated separately and to a limited extent into the west and east of the peninsula, one coming from north-west France and the other from Dorset. The former, who will be designated South-Western Third C used wheel-made cordoned and burnished pottery, including large storage jars and wide-mouthed bowls similar to those found in French hill-forts like Le Petit Celland, Manche, and current there in the time of Julius Caesar. Such pottery was brought to Britain in the first place by Gallic traders, using southern ports like Hengistbury Head, IRON AGE C
INTRUDERS

Plate 74

Mount Batten, or Mounts Bay, whence the little black cordoned pot from Sennen was probably derived. In the late first century B.C. they settled at St Mawgan-in-Pyder, near the tin streams, on a site already occupied by south-western 'B' folk. The small fort was at the end of a spur, enclosed by a single rampart and ditch and with an inturned entrance revetted in timber, and later rebuilt in stone. The earliest wooden huts were 20–30 ft in diameter but not truly circular, with an internal post-ring surrounding a central hearth: the floors were levelled into the hillside and at the back there was an earth bank revetted with stone. Hut A, which was attached to another dwelling, Hut W, was a metalworker's workshop; it had two stone-lined hearths in the centre and a long furnace-pit as well as another in a lean-to outside the back of the hut. Tin ore, a bronze ingot and crucibles were found amid much burning on the floor. A fine decorated bronze shield mount, found rolled up as scrap metal, was probably manufactured here at the turn of the first centuries B.C.–A.D. A wide variety of cordoned jars made in the local clay were in use and were associated with worn decorated B wares in the huts and in gullies underlying them, but also with Romanised wares in the later levels. About A.D. 50–70, perhaps at the time of a Roman advance to the west (p. 140) the entrance to the fort was remodelled, some of the huts rebuilt and three new ones constructed: the settlement then continued until the mid-second century A.D.

Fig. 39

Much cordoned C pottery has been found in recent excavations at the Rumps promontory fort, Polzeath, and sporadically elsewhere in Cornwall and north Devon. At Castle Dore hill-fort it occurred only in the later huts, after the defences and entrance had been remodelled *circa* 50 B.C.

The second group who penetrated into south-east Devon were colonists from the Durotriges of Dorset and Somerset, now known as Southern Third C. They issued coins (p. 130), a large hoard of which was found at Cotley near Axminster

Fig. 39. Bronze shield-mount from Caerloggas hill-fort, St Mawgan-in-Pyder, Cornwall. Scale 1 : 3

and produced wheel-made pottery, of which a bead-rim bowl, often decorated with three ribs and festoons of dots is character-istic. They also used tall cooking pots with upright rims and lattice decoration, jars with counter-sunk lug-handles, mugs and occasionally cordoned and pedestal pottery of Belgic type.

Plate 75

At Hembury, the *oppidum* near Honiton (p. 120) these late Iron Age people reduced the size of the fort by building two transverse ramparts and ditches across the centre and living only in the northern half. The west entrance was blocked but there was a gate to the southern tip of the spur through the new defences. Finds show that the occupation continued until about A.D. 65–70.

Plate 66

129

TRADE AND CURRENCY IN THE LATE IRON AGE

In the mid first century B.C. Julius Caesar broke the sea power of the Veneti and Coriosolites, the Armorican tribes who had become the principal carriers of tin from the south-west (p. 115). Overseas trade in metals thereafter declined, for the Romans had regained the control of the Spanish mines and the supply to the Mediterranean was assured. Its place was taken in some degree, by trade with the neighbouring Celtic confederacies, the Duro-triges of Dorset and south Somerset and the Dobunni of Gloucestershire and north Somerset.

The Durotriges had an *entrepôt* within the large promontory fort on Hengistbury Head, which controlled the Stour and Salisbury Avon waterways. Excavations in 1912 by J. P. Bushe-Fox showed that silver and copper coins were minted here, metals were smelted, shale worked, and several varieties of continental pottery imported in the first centuries B.C. and A.D. The coins were debased copies of the gold stater of Philip of Macedon, which had reached southern Britain from Belgic Gaul early in the first century B.C.; the Durotrigian model was the Gaulish Atrebatic stater (Allen's Gallo-Belgic C.), from which the head and horse designs on obverse and reverse were reduced to a series of dots and squiggles by the native moneyers. Twelve newly minted Durotrigian silver coins were found in the large hoard of Armorican coins at Le Câtillon in Jersey, deposited *circa* 56–51 B.C. showing that the Durotriges were striking in the first half of the first century B.C. Whilst the design of the coins came from the south-east, the metal was derived from the south-west. Analysis of a 19 lb block of silver alloy from one of the furnaces at Hengistbury by Professor Gowland proved it to be derived from an argentiferous copper ore obtainable in the Callington district. Further proof of a Durotrigian trading connection with the Dumnonii comes from Mount Batten, Plymouth where silver coins occur in the settlement and in hoards with others of the Coriosolites.

The Dobunni also traded with the Dumnonii. Their un-inscribed gold and silver staters, with the characteristic triple tailed horse on the reverse and fernlike symbol on the obverse, occur at Mount Batten, and single examples of their inscribed issues of the first century A.D. have been recorded from Plym-outh, Bellever Tor on Dartmoor and Camborne, Cornwall. The trade route was down the Stour to Hengistbury and by the south coast. Its earlier use is shown by finds of iron currency bars, which originated amongst the Western Second B peoples of the Severn-Cotswold area, and reached both Hengistbury and South Devon; a hoard of twelve bars was found at a small hill-fort in Holne Chase, in the same metalliferous district on the Dart as the two Greek silver coins were found (p. 116).

A trading connection with the Belgic settlement in Kent is indicated by the surviving uninscribed coins from two hoards found in 1749 in Carn Brea hill-fort, Camborne, which was well situated to control the tin of Penwith; a single coin of Cunobelin (A.D. 5-40), the Belgic ruler of the south-east, was also found here.

The Dumnonii themselves never achieved a coinage: it is possible that they, like the Masai in East Africa, counted their wealth in cattle and used the beasts to fix a bride-price and as a medium of exchange amongst themselves.

CELTIC ART AND RELIGION

The excellence of decorative metalwork produced by the Celtic peoples in Britain before the Roman conquest is well-known, and it remains to assess the south-western achievements in this respect. There is nothing in the region that can be assigned to the first flowering of insular La Tène art in the third and second century B.C., which developed from continental models in the Waldalgesheim style and was strongly influenced by the clas-sical palmette, seen on the Battersea and Witham shields. The

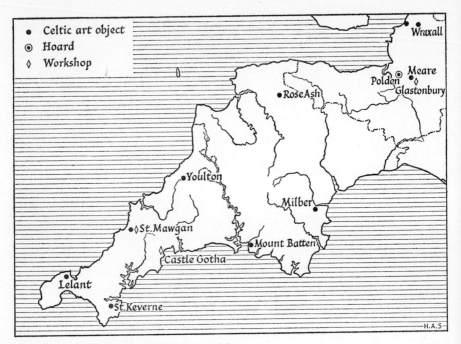

Key:
• Celtic art object
◉ Hoard
◊ Workshop

Wraxall
Meare
Polden
Glastonbury
Rose Ash
Youlton
Milber
St. Mawgan
Mount Batten
Castle Gotha
Lelant
St. Keverne

H.A.S

Fig. 40. Distribution of Celtic art objects and workshops

nearest examples are two minor pieces, the bronze spoons or scoops from Weston near Bath, and the bit-rings from West Coker, Yeovil, which both have derivative spidery designs in low relief. In the peninsula at this time the invasions were in progress, the population unsettled, and neither the craftsmen nor the market for finery stabilised.

The first century B.C. saw the establishment of schools of metal-workers in southern Britain, producing articles for chief-tains and their women decorated in accordance with local tastes and changing fashions. Bronze working in huts at Glas-tonbury and Meare, at Castle Gotha and at St Mawgan-in-Pyder have already been mentioned, which indicate that, like the decoration of pottery, the craft was widespread. It must not be assumed, however, that all metalwork found in the south-

west was made locally; some may be trade goods, others gifts   *Fig. 40*
which have travelled far from their place of origin.

The distribution of fine pieces is scattered with a concentration in north Somerset, an area with a long tradition of bronze
working. The south-west region can claim to be the origin of
the British 'mirror-style', so called from the engraved decoration
on the backs of mirrors found in women's graves both in the
west and the Belgic south-east, *c.* 50 B.C. – A.D. 40. The patterns
are linear, incised in outline on the bronze and some elements
are picked out by hatching or 'basketry' shading as on the pot-   *Fig. 41*
tery. The earliest example is on a sword scabbard found in peat-
cutting on Meare Heath in 1928 and which is dated by its
heart-shaped shape to the late second or early first century B.C.   Plate 76
The design on the locket is balanced but asymmetrical; the
ambiguity between the background and pattern is characteristic. The St Keverne mirror, from a woman's grave in an
inhumation cemetery at Trelan Bahow, in the Lizard, is recognisably in the same style; its two engraved roundels contain
different asymmetrical designs, but composed of the same elements: it probably dates from the middle first century B.C.
The unprovenanced 'Mayer' mirror in the Liverpool Museum
with three linked roundels is of the same queer type and another
early example of this western school; Sir Cyril Fox has shown
that its design is ancestral to the whole of the British mirror
series.

*Fig. 41. Bronze scabbard mount ornament from Meare,
Somerset*

In the last of the south-western mirrors, from the Mount Batten cemetery (Stamford Hill), Plymouth (p. 113) the influence of classical fold-over symmetry of the Augustan era (23 B.C.–A.D. 14) can be detected. It has three roundels, the lower two being identical and the third with a design that is symmetrical about the axis. Fold-over symmetry also governs the satisfying interlocking design of the red enamelled brooch-plate from a hoard of harness fittings and armour found in 1800 on the Polden ridge in Somerset: this unusual piece was probably used to secure a horse's caparison on a ceremonial occasion. Both brooch and mirror reflect the new fashion in Celtic design which developed in the first century A.D.

Plate 77
Fig. 39

The handsome bronze collar from Wraxall, Somerset, and the shield mount from St Mawgan-in-Pyder (p. 128) show the more florid relief decoration, which was practised by another western school in the early first century A.D. Running scrolls and peltas high-lighted with spots of glass or enamel are characteristic motifs, stippling replaces cross-hatching, and a wavy line produced by alternating fine punch marks was often employed. The bronze collar found in a tin stream at Trenoweth,

Plate 78

Lelant, is a product of a less competent craftsman of this school; the decoration consists of stippled peltas flanked by squat trumpet scrolls, which retain their insets of clear and amber glass; the design is a simplification of that on the Wraxall collar. It is made in two parts of thin sheet bronze beaten over and riveted at either end to a lead core. The fastening is uncertain; the analogous Wraxall collar swivels on and fastens by ingenious mortise and tenon joints. Both collars are too heavy for regular wear and probably were for ceremonial use: they may have adorned an image like the torc on the Gallic god from Bouray.

Plates 79, 80

The small wooden idol found in the clay works at Hennock in the lower Teign valley, though not closely dateable, shows that human cult figures were known in the south-west.

Plates 81–84

Two bronze bowls from Rose Ash, north Devon and from

Youlton, north Cornwall may also be associated with religious observances; both were found in bogs and like the famous silver cauldron from Gundestrop, Denmark, or the Llyn Cerrig hoard in Anglesey, were probably votive offerings. The bowls are made of thin beaten bronze with the rims finished by turning on a lathe and decorated by characteristic south-western wavy lines. The Rose Ash bowl has an animal-head escutcheon, probably an ox, Youlton has an inverted human or daemonic head, probably wearing a plumed helmet: they illustrate the Celtic capacity for formalising imagery. The bowls date from the end of the first century B.C. and the beginning of the first century A.D.: two others were found in the rich woman's grave at Bird-lip, Glos. with the fine mirror and grave-goods of 1–15 A.D., whilst others travelled far afield to Keshcarrigan on the Shan-non and to Leq Piekarski in central Poland, where one was placed in a chieftain's grave in the late first century A.D.

Plate 81

Plate 84

CHAPTER VIII

The Roman Canton of the Dumnonii

THE MILITARY IMPACT A.D. 45–75

THE ROMAN ARMIES of the Emperor Claudius reached the south-west at the conclusion of their victorious campaign against the Durotriges and the western Belgic tribes. A task force comprising the Second Augustan Legion and auxiliaries under the command of the *legatus legionis*, the future emperor Vespasian, had stormed some twenty hill-forts, Maiden Castle amongst them, and conquered the Isle of Wight. The Dumnonii probably soon submitted, thus freeing the military command to move north-east against the Dobunni in north Somerset and Gloucestershire with their rear secure. By A.D. 47–48 the conquest of the west country was practically complete, the important silver and lead mining district on the Mendips was occupied and a military road, the Fossway, had been engineered to link up with other army groups away to the north-east. A wide zone of military occupation formed the frontier at this time, extending from the south-coast estuary of the Axe through Cirencester, Leicester and Lincoln to the Humber.

The Fossway itself is a striking example of a Roman road and much of the south-western sector survives and is used by traffic today. Starting from the Axe the road was aligned north-east so as to avoid the Somerset marshes, the fringes of which were crossed on a high *agger* (embankment), at Ilchester. Thereafter it followed a direct course across undulating country to the Avon at Bath, aligned in characteristic long straight stretches from sighting points on hill-tops. A section uncovered at Ilchester showed that it was constructed on a foundation of the local lias rock which had been packed with flinty gravel and lime mortar and surfaced with fine gravel to a width of over 14 ft.

The garrison forts in this sector of the frontier have yet to be discovered; a stamped tile of the Second Augustan legion found at Seaton is almost certainly of second or third century date when the legion is known to be at Caerleon, and does not indicate, as has often been supposed, an early legionary encampment: nevertheless a terminal fort on the Axe estuary to control land and sea traffic is likely. Ilchester where the Fossway is joined by a road from mid-Dorset is another probable site, although the mid-first century settlement excavated within the later Roman town walls appears to be native in character.

After A.D. 47, when Ostorius Scapula succeeded Aulus Plautius, Claudius' first governor and commander-in-chief, the frontier was menaced by the Silures, the Celtic tribes in South Wales, who were skillfully led by Caractacus, the refugee Belgic ruler. An advanced legionary base therefore was established to control the Severn crossing at Gloucester either for the Second Augustan legion or for the Twentieth brought up from Colchester, and it is likely that the military occupied zone was now extended westwards to the Bristol Channel to forestall a Silurian landing on the flank. Sea Mills *(Abonae)* near Avonmouth at which many Claudian coins and some early Samian pottery have been found, was occupied at this time, making a harbour in the Avon available to the fleet. An undated $3\frac{1}{2}$ acres fort at Wiveliscombe, north-west of Taunton has been tentatively assigned to this period.

A watch on the Silures proved to be necessary for the next twenty years until they were finally subdued by Julius Frontinus the governor, in A.D. 74–75. For this purpose two fortlets were built on high points on the Exmoor coast at Martinhoe and Old Burrow on either side of Lynmouth, which command extensive views across the channel to South Wales. Both were strongly defended by double ramparts and ditches with a

Plate 85

third line about 70 ft away forming an outer enclosure. The single entrances were on opposite sides so that if attackers forced the outer gate, they would have to make a half circuit under fire between the defences before reaching the gate of the inner enclosure. The fortlets were built and maintained by troops who probably were landed in the nearby coves on the rocky coast: the isolated garrisons would need to establish friendly relations with the native peoples in the many small hill-forts in the neighbourhood.

Fig. 42

Recent excavations at Martinhoe have shown that this fortlet was occupied in the reign of Nero (A.D. 54–69) and it seems unlikely to have been evacuated before Frontinus' successful

Fig. 42. Reconstructed plan of the Roman fortlet at Martinhoe, north Devon. C ovens; F furnace; G post-holes for gate-posts; P pit

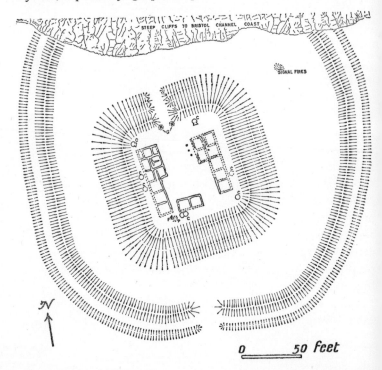

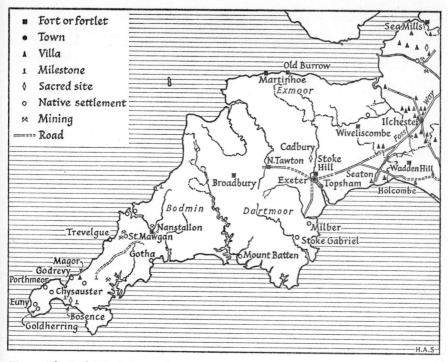

Fig. 43. The South West in Roman times

campaigns of A.D. 74–75. The garrison was a detachment of 80 men (a century), who were housed in two wooden barracks, divided into cubicles with extra rooms in one of them for the officer-in-charge. Their cooking was done in a row of field ovens at the back of the turf rampart; a third building, which had a small domed furnace outside it, was probably for the armourers. Signal fires on the cliff edge in the outer enclosure show how these outposts gave warning of enemy movement across the Bristol Channel, visible from their high vantage points. The signals would be directed to ships of the Roman fleet ready to intercept.

There are some other indications that military activities were extended to the peninsula at this time. Although there are no signs of a fort at Exeter where, as we shall see, a town had been founded, a port at Topsham was in use in pre-Flavian times and could have been a naval supply base. Further west there is a rectangular earthwork at North Tawton which is of the right proportions for a 6½ acre auxiliary fort, and where first century Roman pottery has been found. It is sited to control a crossing of the Tawe and is approached across the claylands by four miles of Roman road on the line of parish boundaries. Continuing westwards there is a possible half-acre fortlet on the crest of Broadbury (800 ft) on a ridge-road aiming to cross the Tamar above Launceston. Bodmin Moor, like Dartmoor, was probably by-passed on its northern flank to reach the coastal plateau. Beyond Bodmin, a square earthwork with double ditches at Nanstallon has produced decorated Samian of Neronian date and three coins of Vespasian (A.D. 69–79): it commands a ford over the Camel and also the nearby tin-workings at Boscarne where first century finds have been recorded. A probing thrust to the west in the sixties or seventies thus is a distinct possibility, designed to open up the peninsula and to prospect for metals, which were imperial property. The re-fortification of the gate of the St Mawgan-in-Pyder hill-fort (p. 128) also in a tin-streaming area not far from Nanstallon may be a native reaction to the advance: the presence of Roman troops in the neighbourhood would explain how the inhabitants acquired some Samian pottery and Romano-British brooches in the late first century A.D.

Fig. 43

THE FOUNDATION AND DEVELOPMENT OF ISCA DUMNONIORUM A.D. 50–55

The Dumnonian people as a whole had remained unaffected by the military campaigns and exploration: since they had shown themselves peaceably inclined, their territory was not occupied at first as was that of the Durotriges and they were

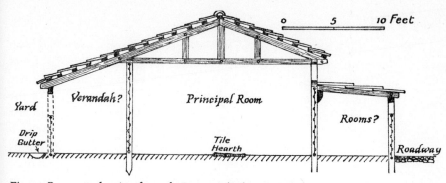

Fig. 44. Reconstructed section of an early Roman timber house in Exeter

encouraged to develop a civilisation and an administration on the Roman pattern. It was the policy of the governor Ostorius Scapula (A.D. 48–52) to form the southern part of Britain that had been easily conquered into an imperial province. A town was therefore founded at Exeter as a social and administrative centre for the Dumnonii. It was sited at the end of a spur leading to the first convenient crossing of the Exe, from which river it took its name of *Isca*, (*Eisca*, in Celtic meaning 'river abounding in fish'). Its population would be drawn from the many hill-forts in the districts, with a sprinkling of foreign merchants and a few officials.

The earliest dwellings which were uncovered in excavations in the city centre from 1945–7, were rectangular timber houses and workshops, regularly aligned on either side of a narrow road leading downhill to the river crossing. They had a frame of stout posts driven into the ground 2–3 ft apart, interwoven walls of wattle and daub and roofs of red Roman tiles made from the local clay. These houses were occupied from A.D. 50–55 until A.D. 75; others, also fronting on to an east to west road, which were found in Bartholomew Street in 1959, were not built till A.D. 65–70, and were destroyed by fire about A.D. 80. Although the buildings themselves were on a modest scale, the inhabitants were using Roman coins freely; they had attractive and varied red Samian tableware imported from South Gaul,

Fig. 44

141

Plate 89

glass cups and beakers from the Mediterranean and other decorative pottery made in Gaul or Germany: oil and wine were
available in imported amphorae. In addition they continued to

Plate 75

use their native coarse pottery including the ribbed bowls current east of the Exe before the conquest. It is evident that the
early township flourished, unaffected by the Boudiccan rebel-
lion in A.D. 60–61 which set back similar developments in the
towns of the south-east.

There was a great change about A.D. 80–85 when the wooden
buildings in the centre were demolished, the site levelled and
public buildings in mortared stone were erected. This is in
accordance with the governor Agricola's known policy of en-
couraging ambitious urban improvements, much in evidence
at Verulamium. Unfortunately only fragmentary foundations
of what were once imposing structures built in the classical style
have survived in Exeter. Part of the open court and ambulatory
belonging to the civic centre, the Forum and Basilica, have
been found in South Street, whilst in the neighbourhood of
the Deanery a large plunge bath, a portico and a stone-lined
conduit indicate the site of the Public Baths. From the second
century onwards, houses were also built in stone, with cement
or tessellated floors, some with simple geometric designs, but
which were only rarely heated by hypocausts. Trade continued
to flourish as shown by the imports of second century Samian
pottery from Lezoux, and by a number of Roman coins with
Greek legends from eastern Mediterranean mints, mostly Alex-
andrian tetradrachms of the third century A.D. when this mint
was prolific in its issues.

Up till the middle of the second century the city, like others
in Britain, was unenclosed and undefended: a rampart and
ditch was then constructed enclosing 92 acres, to which an im-

Plate 87

pressive stone wall was added *circa* 200 A.D. It was built of the
local dark volcanic stone, with a core of grouted rubble 9 ft
thick and a facing of ashlar above a chamfered plinth. Its con-

Fig. 45. Inscriptions of the Dumnonii from Carvoran and Thirwall on Hadrian's Wall

struction, like that of the majority of British town walls was undertaken probably in accordance with an edict of the Emperor Septimius Severus (A.D. 193–211) in consequence of the serious disturbances in the province at the end of the second century. In its heyday, *Isca* must have been an attractive city, unusual in that so much of its interior was on steeply sloping ground with views to the neighbouring hills.

The importance of *Isca* was not only that of a self-contained town in which the pleasures of a civilised life were available to its inhabitants in an attractive and secure urban setting, but, as its name with the tribal suffix implies, it was the administrative centre for the whole of the Dumnonian people, the *Civitas Dumnoniorum*. Under the Roman scheme for the Celtic peoples who had strong tribal loyalities, the Iron Age confederacies were constituted self-governing units, run on the new democratic pattern, each with a principal city. At *Isca Dumnoniorum,* the *ordo* or Council composed of the decurions and their elected magistrates, drawn in the first instance from the tribal chieftains, would discus matters that concerned not only the town but the whole of the peninsula. The Council were responsible for the assessment and collection of taxes throughout the canton, both those levied on the *civitas* by the Imperial procurator on behalf of the central government and those required locally. Two inscriptions on Hadrian's Wall attest a corporate act of the *Civitas Dumnoniorum,* in company of other *civitates,* a contribution in men or money, towards the rebuilding of the northern frontier probably in Severan times.

Fig. 45

Fig. 43

The territory governed from *Isca* extended westward for the length of the Cornish peninsula as is evident from Ptolemy's naming of the Lizard as the Dumnonian promontory. On the east, the boundary with the Durotriges lay in the tumbled-wooded country at the end of the Blackdowns traversed by the Fossway. It then extended north-east from the Parett, for the Somerset river Axe apparently was included in Dumnonian territory by Ptolemy writing in the second century A.D., and as we have seen (p. 126) this district had strong cultural links with the peninsula in the Iron Age. Some adjustment was probably effected in the third century when Ilchester *(Lindinis)* was recognised as a cantonal town of the *Civitas Durotrigensis*, in addition to Dorchester *(Durnovaria)*. The flourishing population in the villas on the land fringing the Somerset marsh in late Roman times must relate to this township, not to *Isca*.

ROADS

Fig. 43

The canton was served by a road system intiated and maintained by the central government, which linked it with the rest of the province. *Isca* was reached by a branch of the Fossway and by a road from Dorchester *(Durnovaria)* of which good stretches are preserved between Axminster and Honiton and at Rockbeare. West of the Exe, a road with *agger* and side ditches has recently been traced over Haldon, which crossed the Teign by a bridge above Newton Abbot to serve south Devon, whilst north of Dartmoor, the length of road at North Tawton already mentioned (p. 140) aimed for the Tamar on its way to the west: as today, Dartmoor compelled a divide in the main roads at Exeter. In Cornwall no constructed roads have been identified with certainty but five milestones of the mid-third and early fourth centuries show that it was included in the system, probably when tin mining was resumed in late imperial times (p. 156). Those at Tintagel and Boscastle and at St Hiliary and Breague are evidence for short lengths on the north and south coast respectively, whilst the Gwennap

Pit milestone of Gordian III, found upright and probably *in situ* near Redruth, could relate to a road down the spine of the narrowing peninsula. Traffic must also have been by sea, principally along the south coast as in prehistoric times. Plate 90

The limited knowledge of the road system prevents us from making use of the road-books to identify the principal places in the canton. The third century Antonine Itinerary mentions *Moridunum,* a town 15 miles from Exeter and 36 from Dorchester, which should be in the Otter valley, whilst the Ravenna Cosmography, a compilation of early road-books in the VIIth century, also mentions it on a route east from Exeter *(Scadummorum)* to Ilchester *(Lindinis).* The Cosmography also contains a string of 14 place-names, mostly unidentifiable, but situated to the west of Exeter; they include *Tamaris,* which must be at a crossing of the Tamar, preceded by *Nemetostatio,* which on the evidence of the present-day *Nymet* names around Bow and North Tawton is probably the North Tawton fort (p. 140): the suffix *statio* implies that it became a tax-collecting centre. A second *statio, Deventiasteno* was probably in South Devon, perhaps at Mount Batten or Plymouth.

A new centre for administration, new building techniques, and a new relationship to a power outside the area fostered by new lines of communication were, then, the principal introductions of Roman rule. To what extent did they affect the life of the Dumnonii and how far did their territory become romanised? There can be no simple answer to these questions. The transition from the Celtic to the Romano-British way of life can sometimes be traced archaeologically when a round hut was replaced by a mortared stone house as at Catsgore in Somerset. Among the Dumnonii the first steps can be seen at Milber, Newton Abbot, where a rectangular enclosure for the wooden buildings of a native farm was erected *circa* A.D. 50 beside an abandoned concentric hill-fort. Similarly the peoples living in Hembury hill-fort (p. 129) moved away about A.D.

ROMAN-STYLE BUILDINGS

Fig. 43

70, after having acquired some Romano-British goods, but their new settlement is undiscovered. Roman-style buildings in the canton are few and with one exception are limited to east Devon; even in the pleasant Exe valley, within easy reach of *Isca* and the new roads, or in the hinterland of Torbay, no villas are recorded, which is puzzling. On Seaton Down, over-looking the Axe estuary, extensive remains of stone buildings with tessellated floors and hypocausts have been uncovered on several occasions: their character is consistent with either a large country-house with outbuildings or with a small township. This may be *Moridunum*, for the Latin place-name appropria-tely means 'the fort by the sea', which in Saxon speech could have become Seaton. But if the distances in the Itinerary are correct *Moridunum* should be ten miles nearer to Exeter.

Other remains of well-built country houses are recorded from Whitestaunton, Combe St Nicholas and Holcombe, all in territory on the Durotrigian border. Holcombe, near Lyme Regis, is distinguished by an elaborate bath suite built in the fourth century A.D. It had an octagonal plunge bath with a tessellated floor and surround, stone columns, corbels and a pendentive decorated with patterns of carved scallop shells, all indicative of a building of some architectural distinction. The bath suite at Lufton, near Yeovil which has an attractive mosaic of fishes surrounding the octagonal plunge is probably the work of the same west-country architect among the Durotriges.

Plate 88

That there was luxurious living in the Roman style in east Devon is shown by the fine bronze mount from a tripod found in 1840 on the beach at Sidmouth: it figures the boy Achilles riding Cheiron the centaur and hunting a wild beast and is a Mediterranean import of the second century A.D. Such tripods supported either bronze bowls or small table tops when the evening meal was served in a well-to-do household.

The one Roman style building remote from *Isca* is the small country house at Magor, near Camborne in west Cornwall,

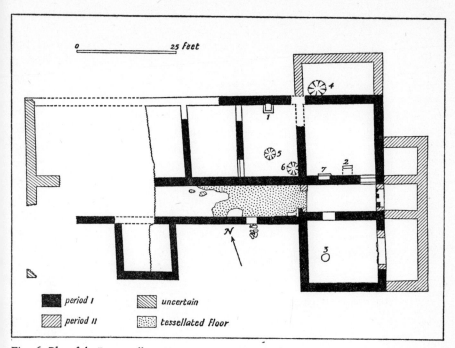

Fig. 46. Plan of the Roman villa at Magor, Camborne, Cornwall. 1–3. hearths; 4–6. pits; 7. wall recess

which was erected in the mid-second century, extended and abandoned in the third century. The house possesses in a crude form most of the novelties in building technique, a slate roof, mortared walls lined with painted plaster, a tessellated floor in the corridor and others of cement or *opus signinum*. Its rusticity is betrayed by its lack of symmetry and by the fact that none of its angles are true: the mason was obviously not acquainted with the rule of Pythagoras. It has been suggested that it was the dwelling of a native of the district who had lived further east, perhaps serving as a decurion in *Isca* or with the army, and who on his return built a house on his estate with local labour in the style which he had become accustomed to see in the town.

Fig. 46

NATIVE-STYLE
BUILDINGS For the majority of the Dumnonii there was little change in their mode of life; they continued to live in small groups in round stone huts and the only signs of contact with the new order is their acquisition of some better made black-cooking pots and dishes, and the occasional coin or trinket. A home-stead at Stoke Gabriel, near Totnes, recently excavated, may be taken as typical; here a small community built a rectangular stone-walled cattle pound on a limestone hill top in the first century A.D. and continued to live in round huts and to till their small lynchetted fields until the middle of the fourth centu-ry. They acquired some Samian and colour-coated wares from a distant market but used mainly rough cooking-pots and storage-jars of local manufacture. In west Cornwall the two small enclosed homesteads of Porth and Crane Godrevy, Gwithian, tell the same story. The pottery and a few late third century coins from the single hut at Port Godrevy show that it was occupied from the second until the fourth century A.D., but the inhabitants had little metal apart from one fine brooch, and were using beach pebbles and stone tools.

Some of the western hill-forts continued to be inhabited; Carn Brea and Trevelgue have both produced late imperial issues as well as first century coins: St Mawgan-in-Pyder (p. 128) and the Round at Castle Gotha (p. 125) continued to be occupied throughout the first and second centuries, without any apparent change in the mode of life.

COURTYARD
HOUSES There is one new development in native architecture in Roman times which is limited to the granitic uplands of Land's End, known to the ancient writers as Belerion: here a house and its outbuildings were built as a single incorporated unit around an open courtyard, from which the type is named. It is best seen at Chysauster, Gulval, a village of eight such houses, arranged in pairs on opposite sides of a street, with two or three more together with an underground store (fogou) a short distance away. The houses are irregular ovals, up to 90 ft

Plate 92

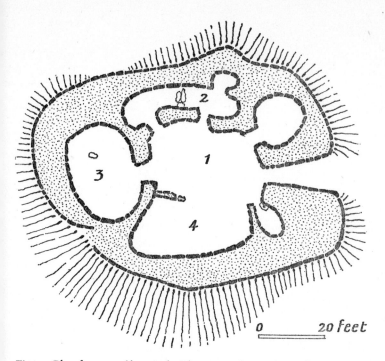

Fig. 47. Plan of a courtyard house in the Chysauster settlement, Cornwall. 1. courtyard; 2. long room; 3. round room; 4. stable

along, terraced into the hillside, with the entrances turned away from the prevailing south-west winds. Across the courtyard was the principal dwelling (3) a round or oval hut with the roof supported on posts set in stone sockets. On one side of the courtyard was a long narrow room (2) which was a work-room, sometimes for industrial purposes, and on the other there was a recess with a lean-to roof (4), probably a stable for ponies. There may also be other small round rooms opening into the courtyard but the round room, long room and courtyard are the constant features of the type. To a certain extent, it reflects the provincial Roman house with its range of separate rooms for different use but the absence of rectangularity shows that it was not a direct copy. Its affinities are more with the round

Fig. 26
Fig. 29

huts at Bodrifty or on Dean Moor which have internal divisions or with the metal-worker's hut at Kestor, with its central opening dividing the living-room from the smithy.

Plate 92

The inhabitants of Chysauster were primarily farmers; there are lynchetted and terraced fields around the settlement. Each house had a small paddock or garden, whilst a sunk road leads down to the stream for watering stock. Some water, however, was brought to the village in slab-covered channels, which also act as drains for surface water in the courtyards. The pottery, mostly native copies of Romano-British types but also a few cordoned sherds (p. 128) indicates an occupation in the first and second centuries A.D. and in some houses until the third, when the village was peacefully abandoned.

There are between thirty and forty examples of these compounds in the Land's End peninsula but they are part of complex village settlements which originated in the Iron Age. At Goldherring, Sancreed, recently excavated, the primary settlement was in round huts enclosed by a wall and ditch, and the courtyard house was secondary being built on a layer of dark soil containing Iron Age pottery. Pottery found included decorated and cordoned Iron Age wares (South-Western Third B and C) and local Romano-British wares, as well as coins of the Gallic emperors of the third century, indicating an occupation from the beginning of the first century A.D. till the end of the fourth. At Portmeor, Zennor, the settlement consisted of seven round huts and two courtyard houses within a walled enclosure of an acre and a second complex, more ruined, with a fogou and another courtyard house lower down the hillside. Here, too, a courtyard house and its associated cultivation terrace were stratigraphically later than the enclosure wall, and were dated by two second century Roman coins, one of Marcus Aurelius (160–180 A.D.) sealed in the lower floor of the Round room. The finds from Portmeor indicate an occupation of over 400 years continuing into the fifth century.

Iron or tin smelting was in evidence at Porthmeor: in the Long Room of one courtyard house there was a stone-edged hearth three feet in diameter, the centre lined with sherds to absorb and retain the heat, which rested on a cone of burnt clay probably from a previous smelt, whilst in the Round room of the second house, there was another pottery-lined hearth with a forging pit beside it, two feet deep and full of fire rakings.

Another feature peculiar to the Land's End settlements is the provision of a *souterrain* or underground chamber, known locally as a *fogou*. These may be entered from one of the courtyard houses as at Carn Euny, Sancreed, or be situated a little distance away as at Chysauster. There are a few fogous built inside small defensible earthworks as at Treveneague, St Hiliary, but they never occur at the large contour or promontory forts. They were constructed by excavating a sloping trench about 5 ft wide and 6 ft deep, lining it with drystone walling which was battered inwards and roofed with flat slabs: the soil from the excavation was heaped on top as at Pendeen Vau or incorporated in the rampart of the enclosure as at Halligey, Trelowarren. The usual plan is a curving gallery with entrances at either end and orientated south-west–north-east, facing the prevailing wind; there may also be shafts and side-chambers as at Boleigh or Carn Euny. At Porthmeor (p. 150) a similar structure was built above ground, curving round the Round room of a courtyard house, and contemporary with it.

The functions of these structures have been much debated: when Hencken wrote in 1932, it was assumed that they were hiding-places, with an emergency exit through the end or side passages in case of trouble, despite the fact that the main entrance is obvious and that the majority would be a death-trap in an attack. It now seems likely they were for domestic use, and were built as communal cellars or cold stores. Food stored in them would be kept at an even temperature, being below ground, in a through draught and free from contamination by

FOGOUS

Plate 93

Fig. 48

151

flies: meat could be dried in them as was done until very recently in passage-like drystone buildings in Shetland, where after the autumn killing, skinned and gutted carcases were hung on stretchers in the drying-house for several months. The ash-pits found at Trewardreva fogou and in the circular side-chamber at Carn Euny probably were for preserving gulls' eggs, as was done on St Kilda until recently. The deep layer of black greasy mould with charcoal, animal and bird bones which covered the floor at Treveneague is also suggestive of a food store. Finally there is the statement of Diodorus Siculus that Iron Age people in Britain stored their grain in 'under-ground repositories', bringing out a little for grinding each day; since this information was derived from Pytheas, it should relate to the south-west and could be applicable to the fogous.

It is apparent from finds of Iron Age pottery (Third B) at Boscaswell, Boleigh and Treveneague and from others of Ro-man character at Carn Euny that the fogous are of pre-Roman origin, but as an essential element in the domestic economy of the Penwith settlements, they continued in use during the Ro-man period. Their limited distribution, which practically coin-cides with that of the courtyard-house, points to a distinctive group of Celtic people in west Penwith, the ancient Belerion. In all probability, they constituted a *pagus*, and as such, be-came one of the territorial subdivisions of the *Civitas Dumno-niorum* when the new social order was established.

SACRED SITES   Some sacred places of the Iron Age survived through Roman times: the Celtic term for a sanctuary or grove, *nimet*, was incor-porated in *Nemetostatio*, a place mentioned in the Ravenna Cosmography and located at North Tawton (p. 140). The element appears in the Doomsday village names in this area and in the Nympton villages near South Molton, in the region where the Rose Ash bowl was found (p. 134). Another name in the *Cosmography*, *Devionissio*, means the place on the holy stream. Although no temples have been discovered, native cult-

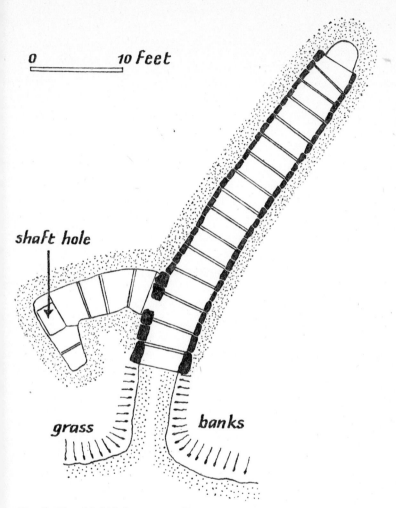

shaft hole

grass   banks

Fig. 48. Plan of Boleigh fogou, Cornwall

centres can be inferred at two hill-top sites. At Cadbury hill-fort in the lower Exe valley, there was a shaft 54 ft deep from which many bronze bracelets, rings and beads of late Roman date were recovered in 1848. There are the sort of personal things that were customary as votive offerings at shrines, as at Woodeaton in Oxfordshire. At Bosence, St Erth, there was a similar shaft 36 ft deep in the corner of a rectangular hill-top enclosure, from which a pewter jug of third to fourth century type and a shallow tin dish were recovered in 1756 with other objects. The dish which has been cut down from a larger vessel has a cursive inscription stating it was dedicated to Mars by Aelius Modestus, and in centre a *Rho* or R in another script. Mars was worshipped as a fertility god as well as a war god by the Celts and the dish was probably used with the jug at a near-by shrine for offerings and libations. Analogous deep shafts or wells were associated with Romano-British temples at Pagan's Hill, Chew Stoke, in Somerset, and at Jordan's Hill, Wey-mouth, where bird bones from sacrifices were in the filling.

Plate 91

TIN MINING
AND
INDUSTRY

The right to mine precious metals was vested in the Emperor in Roman times and the mines were either worked as a state concern, with convict labour under military direction, as at the Dolaucothi gold mine in Wales and probably also in the lead mines on Mendip, or they were leased to private speculators, as in Derbyshire. The profits from mining thus went to the central government and only benefited the canton indirectly, as is apparent from the poverty and backwardness of the south-west.

It is evident that the Romans had advance information about the richness of the argentiferous lead on the Mendips because by A.D. 49 lead ingots, the by-product of silver, were being stamp-ed with the Emperor Claudius' name. This early success prob-ably prompted an attempt by the military to prospect for metals in mid-Cornwall *circa* 60–70 A.D. (p. 140), but there is no suggestion of large-scale mining. The prospectors would find that the natives directed them only to the tin streams, and since the Romans were well supplied with this metal from northern Spain, it was not profitable to work. The Callington deposits of silver (argentiferous copper) which had been utilised in the Iron Age (p. 130) apparently were not discovered.

During the second century the tin was worked by the local inhabitants, as at Castle Gotha (p. 125) where part of an ingot mould was found. When the Spanish mines were exhausted in the mid-third century, the situation was changed and there was a renewed demand for tin in north-western Europe. In particular with the massive production of *antoniniani,* coins of debased metal with a wash of silver, which replaced the *denarius* in the third century, tin was needed in increasing quantities by new mints like Trier set up by the Gallic Emperor Postumus (A.D. 258–268). It was apparently the tin streams of mid-Cornwall that were now worked, not those of West Penwith. The 40 lb tin ingot from Carnanton, St Mawgan-in-Pyder with a worn imperial inscription of the fourth century shows that metal was smelted under official control. Other late Roman finds from the tin streams are a pewter cup from Halviggan, St Stephen-in-Brannel, a late third century coin hoard with a tin or pewter dish from Carnon, Devoran, and some oddments from Treloy, St Columb Minor. More signs of government activity are the repair or making of roads in the mining districts of south Cornwall revealed by the milestones of Gordian III (A.D. 235–240) at Gwennap Pit, of Postumus (A.D. 258–268) at St Hilary, and of Constantine I (A.D. 306–308) at Breague.

Plate 94

Plate 90

The increased number of late third and fourth century coins found in mid and west Cornwall, shows that mining brought some money into the region, though only in small amounts to the native settlements like Goldherring or Godrevy (p. 148). Most of it is found in hoards, like the 1600 found in a pot under a stone near Breague. This phenomenon is not peculiar to Cornwall; the debased *antoniniani* of the Gallic Emperors which make up most of the hoards were repudiated by Aurelian in A.D. 274 and throughout Britain many savings were then abandoned. The fourth century hoards, of which six are recorded in Cornwall, are more significant of the prosperity of the region during the Constantinian epoch.

The increased output of Cornish tin in the late third and fourth centuries was also used for the production of tableware, principally pewter jugs and dishes, composed of tin, alloyed with lead or copper. As in later times, polished pewter was a good substitute for the silver used by the wealthy. Pewter is known to have been made at Lansdown, Bath and at Camerton, an industrial settlement on the Fossway, where stone moulds for a skillet and an oval dish have been found, and where lead from Mendip was accessible. Tin or tin-pewter vessels are likely to have been made nearer the source of supply, like the flagon of 96% tin from Carhayes, south Cornwall, into which 2,500 *antoniniani* of A.D. 250–75 were crammed when it was hidden under some stones beside a creek. The distribution along the south coast indicates that the trade was sea-borne; a flagon from Goodrington was found below the low tide level in Torbay.

SUMMARY

The prosperity of the Dumnonii in Roman times thus was a fitful affair. For the majority the change of rulers affected their way of life very little; they were freed from the demands of their chieftains for labour at fortifications but they had to satisfy those of the tax collectors. So far as the limited evidence goes, provided by fields and fogous, mixed farming remained the basis of their economy: its small scale militated against an increase in population.

The canton as a whole was backward and resistant to change; it was the courtyard house that became the mode in west Cornwall, not the Roman one at Magor. Only at *Isca,* the cantonal town and in east Devon was there any real change in building style and way of life. The prosperity that the revival of tin mining brought in the third and fourth centuries was slight and limited by official control. To realise what the Dumnonii missed, we have only to look at the development of the many country houses, like Low Ham and Frampton with their new mosaics, in the adjoining canton of the Durotriges during the early fourth century.

Fig. 43

Historically and archaeologically little is known about the
fourth century. A small fortified post was set up on Stoke Plate 86
Hill, 5 miles from the centre of *Isca*, probably to give warning
of Saxon or other sea raiders coming up the estuary, perhaps
by Carausius (A.D. 284–86). In the city itself, the later Roman
levels have not survived though the coins series continues to the
time of Magnus Maximus (A.D. 383–88). By then the Forum
was in decay, its surface covered with 6 ins of fine black mould,
and with two rubbish pits dug into it, which contained coins
of A.D. 370–80. The later Theodosian issues (A.D. 388–95)
apparently never reached the city, though they occur in a hoard
near Honiton and in several in north Somerset. Long before
the Emperor Honorius wrote to the cities of Britain to tell them
that henceforth they must fend for themselves, it is apparent
that the mechanism of the *Civitas Dumnoniorum* was running
down. The cantonal organisation in some form survived until
the end of the century and probably into the fifth. C. E. Stevens
has drawn attention to a lady's tombstone from Salona, the
Roman town near Split on the Adriatic. Her name is missing
but she was described as CIVIS DUMNONIA when she died, aged
30, in A.D. 425. Her other epithet CLARISSIMA FEMINA shows
that she had married into one of the wealthy senatorial families.
The inscription implies a secure world with freedom of movement and a stable society; in reality the ordered Roman way of
life by this time was changing, both at the centre and on the
periphery of the western Empire as in Dumnonia.

CHAPTER IX

The Dark Ages to A.D. 700

IN A.D. 410 HONORIUS Emperor of the West wrote to the *civitates* of Britain to tell them, in answer to an appeal for military aid, that henceforth they must fend for themselves; each canton now had to rely on its own resources. In eastern England this sub-Roman epoch of independence was brief, lasting only till the influx of Anglo-Saxon settlers from A.D. 450 onwards. In the south-west, as in Wales, it was prolonged, lasting in Devon and West Somerset until the end of the seventh century when the west Saxon king Centwine 'drove the Britons as far as the sea' (A.D. 682) and in Cornwall until the ninth or tenth century when first King Egbert (A.D. 823–39) and finally King Athelstan (A.D. 924–39) overcame Celtic resistance. Here the Celtic society that developed in consequence of the end of Roman rule will be briefly examined as far as the limited archaeological material permits, and we shall take leave of Dumnonia at the beginning of the Saxon attacks.

MEMORIAL STONES

The principal source of information are the memorial stones; the earliest consist of an undecorated slab or pillar on which has been cut in Roman capitals the name of an individual, his parentage and the Latin formula *hic iacit,* he lies here, or *hic in tumulo iacit,* he lies here in the grave, or occasionally *Memoria,* the memorial of; the preceeding name is usually in the genitive case. Memorials of the late sixth or early seventh century can be distinguished by the increasing number of letters in cursive or half-uncial script that derive from contemporary Gallic epigraphy. Despite the formulae, it is rare to find a grave below the stone; the best authenticated is at Hayle, where the fifth century memorial of CVNAIDE was found in 1843 beside a grave containing ashes and charcoal, which was covered by loose stones.

Fig. 49. The Ogam alphabet

The inscriptions show that the memorials are related to Roman tombstones and reflect the Roman social order, Cunaide's
epitaph records that she lived for 33 years and is aligned horizontally in the Roman manner. The names of the people
commemorated are often recognisably Roman, like IVSTVS at
St Kew, LATINUS at Worthyvale or of Roman descent like
the Celtic VLCAGNVS son of SEVERVS from Nanscowe, and
CAVVDVS son of CIVILIS from Lynton. At Buckland Monachorum, DOBVNNVS is described as a smith *(faber),* at Rialton
another person as child of a tribune, presumably a late Roman
official, whilst on the worn stone on Sourton Down, Okehampton, AVDETVS is termed *Princeps.* This title was used by some
barbarian rulers in imperial times, but also by Frankish and
Burgundian kings in the sixth century.

It is evident that Latin retained its prestige along with the
Roman tradition, even if the masons were unsure of their declensions and spelling. Nevertheless it is the Celtic names that
predominate roughly three to one and it is not uncommon
for two generations to have Celtic names like DVNOCATVS the
son of MERCAGNVS at Lancarffe. The name is lost of the man
who was grandson *(Nepos)* of CARATACVS, a famous name in
early Celtic history, on the memorial which stands on Winsford Hill in west Somerset. Women too were occasionally
commemorated like NONNITA on the Tregoney stone or
CUNAIDE (Cunaida) at Hayle.

Plate 95

The Celtic population included some Irish settlers, Goidels
or Q Celts: this is shown by their names and lineage cut in
Ogams along the edges of their memorial stones. The Ogam
alphabet was developed in southwest Ireland in the late third

Fig. 49

or fourth century A.D.; the twenty letters consist of combinations of one to five strokes cut at varying angles on either side of the arris or edge of the stone. Normally the Ogams render either the same name as the Latin, as on the stone of VLCAGNVS, or its Celtic equivalent as *Igenavi* for INGENVI (Ingenvvs) both on stones at Lewannick. On the Fardel, Ivybridge, stone, the Celtic word *Maqvi* (Mac, son of), is used in the original Ogams, SVAQQVCI MAQI QICI, both Irish names and in the secondary Latin inscription of FANONVS MAQVI RINI; a third name, SAGRANVS, was added in the early seventh century. The stone thus commemorated three people of Irish descent.

Plate 96

Plate 97

The memorials in general are those of local rulers and dyn, asties, and indicate that Celtic society had reverted to the aris, tocratic pattern of the Iron Age. Princeps Audetus has already been mentioned; CVMREGNVS at Southhill embodies a royal title; RIALOBRANVS on the Men Scryfys pillar at Madron means 'Royal Raven' whilst CVNOMORVS, whose son DRV, STAVS' memoral was set up on the ridgeway near Castle Dore, Fowey, has been plausibly identified with the *Marcus dictus Quonomorus*, mentioned in the ninth century life of St Paul Aurelian, and with the King Mark of the Tristan legend. From such local rulers emerged the kings or overlords of historic times, including the tyrant Constantine whom Gildas in the mid sixth century named with such vituperation and King Geraint who fought with Ine of Wessex in A.D. 710.

These rulers were nominally Christian: this is evident from the formulae and from the occasional carving of the Chi, Rho, a monogram formed out of the Greek initial letters of Christ (XP), such as can be seen on the memorial of SENILVS at St Just in Penwith or of BROCAGNVS at St Endellion. The Christian symbols *Alpha* and *Omega* also were used. The faith was introduced into the south, west in the fourth century as throughout the Empire generally; there were poor Chris, tians in Exeter who used a black cooking, pot marked with a

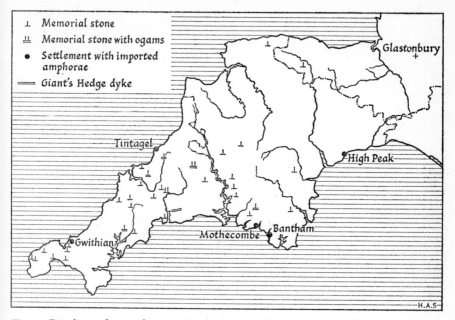

Fig. 50. Distribution of memorial stones and imported pottery of the V-VII centuries A.D.

Chi-Rho. The monogram on the stones, however, with the crooklike *Rho* is a Gallic form and from this and other epigraphic evidence it appears that Celtic Christianity was nurtured by contact with western and southern Gaul after the break-down of Roman control in Britain.

The distribution of the stones is predominantly in the western half of the peninsula with two on Exmoor: during the fifth and sixth centuries it is evident that power shifted away from its Roman centre at *Isca*, which, as we have seen, was a city in decay in the late fourth century and ill-equipped to maintain control of the distant parts of the canton. The Ogam stones indicate fifth century Irish settlements in south-west Devon and in north Cornwall, perhaps coming from south wales,

Fig. 50

where an invasion by the Deisi, a tribe from Waterford, is known to have take place in late Roman times and where memorials in Ogam are frequent, and several of the same Irish names are found. It was customary to set up the stones in isolation, not in churchyards, and often on the roadside in the Roman manner. The ancient route across the peninsula from Padstow to Fowey has three stones sited on it, including the Castle Dore stone, and the stones on Winsford Hill and Sourton Down are both on ridgeways: similar isolated roadside siting occurs in south Wales. It was, however, by the seaways that Dumnonia maintained contact with the surviving Roman and Celtic civilisation in Gaul and the Mediterranean.

SETTLEMENTS, POTTERY AND THE WINE TRADE

Until very recently nothing was known of the places where these people named on the stones lived: their recognition began with the discovery in 1940 at a hill-fort at Garranes in southern Ireland of sherds of foreign wine jugs and amphorae in association with Irish metalwork of sixth century date. Similar wares were subsequently recognised in the south-west, first at the monastic site at Tintagel and then at Bantham, south Devon and Gwithian in Cornwall: in all twelve sites are now known in the south-west and in south Wales. Three main varieties of pottery were imported, all wheel-made; first, little dark red bowls, some with a cross or other motif impressed on the interior (Class A), secondly combed or corrugated amphorae in white or buff ware (Class B), which form the bulk of the sherds in the south-west, and thirdly bowls, jars and small beakers in hard grey ware (Class E). The first two groups originate in the eastern Mediterranean in the fifth century, close parallels having been found as far away as Antioch and Constantinople, with others also distributed in the western Mediterranean; the grey (E) ware is held to come from the Rhineland. All three varieties are found at Gwithian where the stratigraphical evidence indicates that A and B are the earlier, dating from fifth and sixth century, and E is sixth and seventh century or later.

Fig. 50

Fig. 51

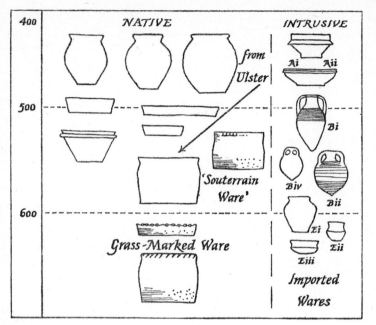

Fig. 51. Dark Age pottery styles of the V-VII centuries A.D.

The trade route from the eastern Mediterranean was through the straits of Gibraltar, and up the Atlantic coast. The preponderance of amphorae and jugs shows that the merchant-venturers were carrying wine and, judging by the occasional residue, olive oil, which was needed for lighting as well as for cooking. Some fine glass from Egypt was sometimes included in the cargo and in the case of the Rhenish merchants, from the Merovingian factories at Cologne, all tempting luxuries for British princes. The landing places were at the mouth of rivers like Bantham on the Avon or Mothecombe on the Erme where there are sheltered anchorages, sandy shores where a boat could be beached, and ridgeways to the hinterland. Remains of fires, piles of shells and animal bones found with the potsherds in black layers under the dunes are all that remain of the encampments of the merchants or their customers. It may be supposed that the boats made the return journey loaded with a profitable cargo; there is the well-known story in the life of John the Almsgiver, patriarch of Alexandria, (A.D. 611–619) of the merchant ship sailing from Egypt to Britain with corn which relieved a famine and returning with a cargo of tin.

At Gwithian a permanent native settlement of this period has been located to the south of the Bronze Age site (p. 92) on the edge of an old tidal creek. It began in the fifth century as a single family hut, with the inhabitants using hand-made dishes and jars, homely copies of Romano-British originals, and acquiring some amphorae of imported wine. During the sixth century the hut was replaced by three others each about 10–12 ft in diameter, with turf walls on a stone foundation. Rubbish from both periods was deposited in pits or on a midden, and shows that a lot of shellfish were eaten as well as beef, mutton and pork: bird and fish bones were strewn on the hut floors. Iron was worked and small fields were cultivated on the sandy soil. The pottery now used included coarse, straight-sided pots, with nicked or fingered rims and on the base impressions of chopped grass or straw, on which the pots had been stood to dry before firing. This device was to prevent the clay sticking to its resting place and was used in Cornwall until the eleventh century; it probably originated in northern Ireland in the sixth century where similar pottery has been found in souterrains and settlements. Sherds of imported amphorae and of wheel-made Rhenish pots were associated with the grass-marked wares at Gwithian, showing that this modest homestead participated in the trade overseas.

There are signs that several hill-forts were re-occupied at this time, although there is as yet no evidence that new ones were built like Dinas Powys in south Wales. Sherds of amphorae have been picked up after ploughing in the interior of Cad-

Fig. 51

bury Castle, a large multivallate fort in east Somerset; at High Peak, Sidmouth, a fort which has been heavily eroded, a layer of rubbish thrown on to the inner rampart and into the ditch contained similar sherds, whilst at Chun, in Cornwall, (p. 123), a grass-marked pot and an amphora sherd have been recognised from one of the huts behind the rampart. Finally at Castle Dore hill-fort there is a series of stone packed post-holes be-longing to rectangular buildings which were stratigraphically later than those of the Iron Age round huts. The excavator, Mr Ralegh Radford, suggested that these belonged to a large aisled hall, 90 by 40 ft, with a central ridge support, a square kitchen adjoining and another hall 65 by 25 ft, but the evidence is inconclusive, all floors having been destroyed by ploughing. No imported amphorae were found here and the post-Roman date depends archaeologically on a yellow bead which is not closely dateable and two sherds of a jar or bowl of wheel-made grey pottery. The ascription to the sixth century gains some support from the nearby memorial of Drustaus, son of Cuno-morus (p. 160) and from place-names which point to this area as the scene of the King Mark and Tristan story.

Plate 69

Although Christianity started in Dumnonia in late Roman times, its spread to the Celtic population generally in the sixth century was due to missionary monks coming from other Celtic lands, principally from South Wales but also from Ireland and Brittany. This is known because unlike the English custom whereby new churches were dedicated to an appropriate apostle like St Peter, the Celtic churches took the name of their founder who had converted the district and often settled there on land granted by the local ruler. In Cornwall alone, 174 out of the 212 ancient parishes are dedicated to a western saint and about 50 in Devon. By a critical study of the dedications combined with the written lives, which survive mostly in medieval manu-scripts and incorporate a number of obvious inventions, some idea of the conversion can be obtained.

SAINTS AND
MONASTERIES

The initial impulse came from South Wales: at Llantwit Major, Glamorgan, St Iltyd had founded a monastery and a school of learning in the late fifth century from which a succession of powerful personalities crossed the Bristol Channel to evangelise in the peninsula. In the first life of St Samson, (*c*. A.D. 480–560) written at his Breton foundation at Dol as early as the seventh century, there are details of the Welsh saint landing near Padstow, encountering monks from a previous mission at St Kew *(Docco)* and travelling overland with a wagon loaded with sacred books and holy vessels. In the nearby district called *Tricurium* (now Trig Major) he saw the pagan people dancing and worshipping a stone idol and a young man racing on a horse with their chief *(comes)* watching the ceremony, a fascinating survival of rites from prehistoric times: it is alleged that the saint cut a cross on the standing stone after remonstrating with them. At the end of his mission, Samson re-embarked probably from Fowey for Dol in Brittany. Cornwall had also been a halfway house for St Paul Aurelian, who was born in Glamorgan, studied at Llantwit and came by the same trans-peninsular route to King Mark Cunomorus before proceeding to Ushant and Saint Pol de-Léon. St Petroc, a contemporary of Samson, remained in Cornwall, founding his first monastery near Padstow and later moved to Bodmin to land given by the local rulers *(reguli)*, Theodorus and Constantine, in the mid sixth century. Other dedications attest missions by those of Welsh descent to mid and east Cornwall and north Devon, whilst the Irish, like St Breaca of Breague or St Hya who gives her name to St Ives, were principally concerned with west Cornwall. There are also dedications to saints from Brittany, like St Winwaloe of Landévennec at Gunwalloe, St Corentin of Quimper at Cury in the Lizard whilst relics of St Rumon (Ronan of Locronan) were translated from Ruan Lanihorne on the Fal to Tavistock in the twelfth century, although no record has survived in the literature of missions by these saints to Britain.

The settlements of the missionaries were primitive, consisting of a little church or oratory, and cells for the individual monks which were merely huts, such as St Paul Aurelian is recorded to have built beside a spring on Ushant or such as survive on the islands off the west coast of Ireland. There was a strong desire in the Celtic Church to withdraw from the world to the wild places, just as the Theban monks of Egypt had withdrawn to the desert, following the example of saints Paul and Antony in the fourth century. This is well exemplified by the site chosen for the early monastery at Tintagel on an exposed cliff-ringed promontory, now practically an island, 250 ft sheer above the Atlantic. The monks lived in small contiguous rectangular cells, poorly built of stones and clay, with beaten earth floors and thatched roofs. The main complex clusters round the Norman chapel, which has replaced the original church, and the graveyard containing the founder's tomb, or *leacht,* a masonry foundation five feet square. There are other groups of cells on a shelf on the east side of the headland as well as a long narrow building with internal seating identified as the *scriptorium.* There is also a little chamber with a burnt paved floor which was probably a sweat house, in which water was thrown on heated stones to provide a vapour bath. On the northern cliff-edge there was a corn-drying kiln, evidence of inland cultivation. The monastery was founded in the early sixth century, probably by St Julian or Juliot, one of the children of Brychan, from south Wales and there were three or four building periods before it was deserted in the ninth century. There were cells for about 30 monks: their life must have been harsh and poverty-stricken in this wild setting: nervertheless they obtained amphorae of wine and oil, needed for the services, from the foreign merchants.

Plate 98

In contrast to Tintagel, the majority of Celtic churches are on sheltered sites and in touch with the local population. St Petroc's monastery at Bodmin was at the head of a valley which winds down to the wooded gorge of the Camel and was situated on fertile land occupied in the Iron Age from the evidence of the nearby Carnyke hill-fort. At Gunwalloe in the Lizard, St Winwaloe's church, now isolated beside the cove, is close to a cliff-castle; later grass-marked and bar-lug pottery found a short distance away is evidence of continuity of settlement, as is the manor farm of Winnianton, which gave its name to the Hundred in late Saxon times. Other sites favoured are the ends of spurs as at Petrockstow, but the high ground was avoided; wooded valleys were sometimes chosen for a hermitage as at Landkey, and clearing thus initiated. Unlike Wales or Ireland, the original churches have not survived; the little oratory of St Perran, now wrecked and isolated in the dunes behind Perranporth, probably retains its original form and incorporates some pre-Norman masonry. The first church at Glastonbury, the *Vetusta Ecclesia,* is known from William of Malmesbury's account to have been a wooden structure with wattlework 60 ft long by 26 ft wide; it was standing when King Ine of Wessex built his stone church in the Kentish style to the east of it *circa* 700 A.D., and remained until destroyed by fire in 1184 A.D.

SUMMARY   These glimpses of Dumnonia in the fifth and sixth centuries show a land peopled and ruled by Celts, mainly of Romano-British descent and proud of their lineage and limited knowledge of Latin. There were also others newly arrived from Ireland and south Wales who spoke Goidelic and introduced the Ogam script. So far as the meagre evidence goes, their mode of life differed little from that in the Iron Age. Contact with the outside world was by the western seaways, with traders from the Mediterranean, reminiscent of early Bronze Age times, and with compatriots in Wales, Ireland and Brittany, all places linked culturally with the peninsula in megalithic and Iron Age times. The motive that impelled the people across the sea was no longer a search for land to settle but the desire to spread the Christian gospel. With Brittany the link was especially strong. Britons from southern England had migrated there in the face of the Saxon invasions after A.D. 450 and others from the west country , including east Devon, must have followed with the West Saxon advance to the Cotswolds in A.D. 567. By the mid-sixth century there were so many that the peninsula was referred to by Gregory of Tours as Britannia instead of by its Roman name of Armorica. Another sign of the migration is that the Breton and Cornish languages remained closely akin.

Although the south-west was never wholly depopulated, the political cohesion gained during four centuries of Roman rule was lost; as we have seen, the Dark Ages was an era of petty kings and independent local dynasties, of individual saints and independent monasteries. Therefore, when the time came, Dumnonia was ill-equipped to offer effective resistance to the West-Saxons.

Field Monuments to Visit

A representative selection has been made from those which are not too difficult of access and which are well preserved. Sites are arranged topo graphically, in chronological order. Those marked * are in charge of the Ministry of Works, + of the National Trust. Permission should be asked of the owner before visiting others on private property.

West Cornwall

+	Lanyon Quoit, Madron, chamber tomb	SW 430337
	Zennor Quoit, chamber tomb	SW 469380
*	Carn Gluze, St Just, Entrance Grave	SW 353315
	Pennance, Zennor, Entrance Grave	SW 448376
	Merry Maidens stone circle and the	SW 433245
	Pipers' standing stones, Rosmodres	434248
	Chun Castle, Morvah, hill-fort	SW 405339
+	Treryn Dinas, St Levan, promontory fort	SW 398220
+	Trencrom, Lelant, hill-fort	SW 518362
*	Chysauster, Gulval, native village	SW 473350
*	Carn Euny, Sancreed, native village and fogou	SW 402289
	Men Scryfys, Madron, memorial stone	SW 427353

For other monuments, see *Antiquities of the Land's End district*, West Corn wall Field Club Guide No. 2.

East Cornwall

	Pawton, St Breocke, chamber tomb	SW 966697
*	Trethevy, St Cleer, chamber tomb	SX 259689
	Castilly, Lanivet, henge	SX 031629
*	The Hurlers, Linkinhorne, stone circles	SX 258714
	Rillaton, Linkinhorne, barrow	SX 260719
	Taphouse, Braddock, barrows	SX 146633
		175632
	Harlyn Bay, St Merryn, cemetery	SW 878754
	Castle-an-Dinas, St Columb, hill-fort	SW 945625

Hall Rings, Pelynt, multiple enclosure fort   SX 214555
Trevelgue, Newquay, promontory fort   SW 825630
Castle Dore, Golant, hill-fort   SX 103548
*   Tintagel Celtic monastery   SS 050890
Lewannick church, Ogam memorial stones   SX 275808

For other monuments see *Antiquities of the Newquay-Padstow district* West Cornwall Field Club Guide No. 7.

Dartmoor and South Devon

Corringdon Ball, South Brent, chamber tomb   SX 670613
Scorhill, Gidleigh, stone circle   SX 655873
Shoveldown, Chagford, stone rows   SX 650860
Merrivale stone rows and circle   SX 534748
Grimspound, Manaton, enclosed settlement   SX 700809
Kestor, Chagford, huts and fields   SX 665867
Trowlesworthy Warren, enclosed settlements   SX 574645
Butterdon Hill, Harford, cairns and stone row   SX 660587

For other Dartmoor sites, see *Dartmoor National Park Guide.*

Farway barrows   SY 151960
Hembury, Honiton, hill-fort   ST 101030
Milber Down, Newton Abbot, multiple-enclosure fort   SX 885698
\+   Bolt Tail promontory fort   SX 670397
Exeter, Roman city wall, Southernhay and Northernhay Gardens.
Tavistock, memorial stones in the vicarage garden.   SX 480744

North Devon and West Somerset

Five Barrows, Exmoor   SS 732368
Chapman barrows, Parracombe   SS 695435
Clovelly Dykes, multiple-enclosure hill-fort   SS 311235
Countisbury promontory fort   SS 741995
Worlebury, Weston-super-Mare, hill-fort   ST 317625
Old Burrow, Countisbury, Roman fortlet   SS 788495
Winsford Hill, memorial stone   SS 890335

For other Exmoor sites see *Exmoor National Park Guide.*

Museums

Cornwall

Truro. The Royal Institution of Cornwall's museum; a well-arranged collection from the county, including finds from excavations at Knacky-boy, Scilly, Crig-a-Mennis barrow, St Mawgan-in-Pyder hill-fort, and Tintagel Celtic monastery.

Penzance, Penlee House; a small collection of Cornish Bronze Age pottery.

Harlyn Bay, near Padstow; finds from the Iron Age cemetery.

Devon

Exeter. The Royal Albert Memorial museum: finds from Hembury neo-lithic settlement and hill-fort, Farway barrows, Kestor and Dean Moor Dartmoor settlements; Roman remains from Exeter (since 1945) and Holcombe villa.

Plymouth. The City Museum and Art Gallery: Bronze Age pottery from Dartmoor settlements: finds from Mount Batten.

Torquay. The Torquay Natural History Society's museum: finds from excavations at Hazard Hill neolithic settlement, Milber Down hill-fort and Bantham Dark Age settlement.

Somerset

Taunton. The County Museum at Taunton Castle contains a well-ar-ranged collection from Somerset including the Wick barrow, Bronze Age ornament hoards, the Shapwick boat, Meare Lake village and the Low Ham mosaic.

Glastonbury (summer only). Lake village material.

London. The British Museum (sub-dept. of Prehistory and Roman Bri-tain). The Rillaton cup, Morvah and Towednack gold hoards, Rose Ash bowl, Lelant collar, Polden Hill hoard, Fardel memorial stone.

Bristol. The City Museum. The Wraxall torc.

Oxford. The Ashmolean Museum. The Crediton hoard, Bosence Roman pewter.

Bibliography

Abbreviations

ANT. J.	*The Antiquaries Journal.*
ARCH. J.	*The Archaeological Journal.*
ARCH.	*Archaeologia.*
INST. OF ARCH.	*Institute of Archaeology, London University.*
J. BRIT. ARCH. ASS.	*Journal of the British Archaeological Association.*
J.R.S.	*Journal of Roman Studies.*
J.R.I.C.	*Journal of the Royal Institution of Cornwall.*
MED. ARCH.	*Journal of Medieval Archaeology.*
NUM. CHRON.	*Numismatic Chronicle*
P.D.A.E.S.	*Proceedings of the Devon Archaeological Exploration Society.*
P.P.S.	*Proceedings of the Prehistoric Society.*
P.SOM.A.S.	*Proceedings of the Somerset Archaeological and Natural History Society.*
P.W.C.F.C.	*Proceedings of the West Cornwall Field Club.*
T.D.A.	*Transactions of the Devonshire Association.*

General Works

BORLASE, W. C., *Naenia Cornubiae* (1872).
DOBSON, D.P., *Archaeology of Somerset* (1931).
HENCKEN, H. O'N., *Archaeology of Cornwall and Scilly* (1932)
WORTH, R. H., *Dartmoor* (1953).
VICTORIA COUNTY HISTORY. *Cornwall, Devon, and Somerset* (1906–24).
   Articles, of varying merit, on Early Man, Stone circles, Ancient
   earthworks, Romano-British remains, Early Christian monuments.
Arch. J. CXIV (1957) Exeter meeting p. 126 *et seq.*

CHAPTER I

CLAYDEN, A. W., *The history of Devonshire Scenery,* (1906).
DEWEY, H., *British Regional Geology, South-West England.* 2nd edition,
   (1948).

DINES, H. G., *The Metalliferous Mining Region of South-West England*, (1956).

NORTH, F. J., *The Evolution of the Bristol Channel*, (1929).

WELCH, F. B. and KELLAWAY, G. A., *British Regional Geology, Bristol and Gloucester district*, (1948).

CHAPTER II

BOUSFIELD, P. and S., A notable Cornish henge monument (Castilly). *P.W.C.F.C.* I (1953-4) p. 35.

FOX, A., The Castlewitch Ringwork, *Ant. J.* XXXII (1952) p. 67.

GODWIN, H., Prehistoric trackways of the Somerset levels. *P.P.S.* 1960 p. 1.

GRIEG, O. and RANKINE, W.F., A Stone Age settlement system near East Week, *P.D.A.E.S.* V, (1953), p. 8.

HOULDER, C. H., A Neolithic settlement on Hazard Hill, Totnes. *P.D.A.E.S.* no. 21 (1963), p. 2.

LIDDELL, D.M., Excavations at Hembury Fort, Devon. 4 reports, 1930, 1931, 1932, 1934-5, *P.D.A.E.S.* I, p. 40, 90, 162, II, p. 135. Details of the Neolithic occupation will be found principally in the third and fourth reports, the pottery in the second and fourth reports. Radio-carbon dates, A. Fox, *Antiquity* 1963, p. 228

MEGAW, J.V.S., The Neolithic period in Cornwall, *P.W.C.F.C*.II (1957-8) p. 13.

PIGGOTT, S., *Neolithic Cultures of the British Isles* (1954) Ch. 2 and 3.

SIMMONS, I.G., The vegetation history of Dartmoor, *T.D.A.* 94 (1962) p. 555.

STONE, J. F. S. and WALLIS, F. S., The petrological determination of stone axes. 1st Report, *P.P.S.* (1941), p. 50, 2nd report, *P.P.S.* 1947, p. 47, 3rd report, *P.P.S.* 1951, p. 99.

EVENS, E.D., GRINSELL, L. V., PIGGOTT, S. and WALLIS, F.S., 4th Report, *P.P.S.*, 1962, p. 209.

THOMAS, A.C., Carn Brea finds in Camborne Public Library, *Cornish Archaeology* I (1962) p. 104. See also Patchett, F.M. *Arch. J.* CI (1944) p. 20 for other pottery from this site.

WLLOCK, E.H., A Neolithic site on Haldon, *P.D.A.E.S.* II (1936) p. 244. A further note on Haldon. *Ibid.* III (1937) p. 33.

Woods, G.MacAlpine, A Stone Age site in East Devon (Beer Head) *P.D.A.E.S.* I (1929) p. 10.

CHAPTER III

Borlase, W.C., Typical specimens of Cornish barrows. *Arch.* XLIX (1886), p. 181. Includes Entrance Graves at Tregaseal, Chapel Carn Brea and Carn Gluze (Ballowal). See also *Naenia Cornubiae*.

Daniel, Glyn E., *The Prehistoric Chamber-tombs in England and Wales* (1950). South-western tombs are listed on p. 236–50.

Hencken, H.O'N., *The Archaeology of Cornwall and Scilly* (1932) Ch. 2. Great stone monuments.

O'Neil, B.St J., The excavation of Knackyboy cairn, St Martin's, Scilly. *Ant. J.* XXXII (1952) p. 21.

Radford, C.A.R. The chambered tomb at Broadsands, Paignton. *P.D.A.E.S.* V (1957–8) p. 147.

CHAPTER IV

Ashbee, P., The excavation of Tregulland Barrow, Treneglos. *Ant. J.* XXXVIII (1958) p. 174.

Borlase, W.C., *Naenia Cornubiae*, p. 104 for burials beside menhirs.

Brailsford, J., Bronze Age stone monuments of Dartmoor. *Antiquity* (1938) p. 444. Contains plans of stone rows.

Dartmoor Exploration Committee, Exploration of barrows and stone circle at Fernworthy. *T.D.A.* XXX (1898) p. 107.

Dudley, D. and Patchett, F.M., Excavations on Kerrow farm, Zennor: the long-stone site. *P.W.C.F.C.* I (1953–4) p. 44.

Giot, P.R., *Brittany* (1960). Contains the most accessible account of comparable Breton monuments.

Gray, H.StG., Report on the Wick barrow excavations *P. Som. A. S.* LIV (1908) p. 1.

Gray, H.St G., The Stone Circles of East Cornwall. *Arch.* LXI (1909) p. 1.

Piggott, S., Abercromby and after, in *Culture and Environment,* essays presented to Sir Cyril Fox, edited I. Foster and L. Alcock, (1963), p.53. Up-to-date account of the Beaker peoples.

Radford, C.A.R., The Hurlers, Cornwall, Notes on Excavations. *P.P.S.* 1935 p. 134, 1938 p. 319.

Rogers, E. H., Report on the Yelland Stone Row, *P.D.A.E.S.* I (1932) p. 201. The sites at Westward Ho and Yelland. *Ibid.* III (1946) p. 109.

Thomas, A. C., A new cist from Trevedra Common, St Just-in-Penwith. *P.W.C.F.C.* II (1960–61) p. 189.

Worth, R. H., *Dartmoor,* (1953). Stone rows p. 202, Stone circles p. 248. For Beakers see Barrows and Kistvaens, p. 192.

Williams, A., Bronze Age barrows on Charmy Down, Somerset. *Ant. J.* XXX (1950) p. 34.

CHAPTER V

Ashbee, P., Some Wessex barrow forms in South west England. *P.W.C.F.C.* I (1955–6) p. 132.

Ashbee, P., *The Bronze Age round barrow in Britain* (1960).

ApSimon, A. M., Cornish Bronze Age Pottery. *P.W.C.F.C.* II (1957–1958) p. 36.

ApSimon, A. M., Dagger graves in the Wessex Bronze Age. *Institute of Archaeology. Tenth Annual Report,* p. 37. Defines the two phases of the Wessex culture.

Benton, S., The Pelynt Sword-hilt. *P.P.S.* 1952, p. 237.

Childe, V. G., Bronze dagger of Mycenaean type from Pelynt, Cornwall. *P.P.S.* 1951, p. 95.

Crawford, O. G. S., The ancient settlements at Harlyn Bay. *Ant. J.* I (1927) p. 288, for the barrows and lunulae at Harlyn.

Fox, A., The Broad Down (Farway) necropolis and the Wessex culture in Devon. *P.D.A.E.S.* IV (1948) p. 1.

Fox, A. and Stone, J. F. S., A necklace from a barrow at North Molton, Devon. *Ant. J.* XXXI (1951) p. 25.

Hawkes, C. F. C., The double axe in prehistoric Europe. *Annals British School at Athens* XXXVII (1937) p. 141.

Hawkes, C. F. C. and Smith, M., *Inventaria Archaeologica,* Great Britain, II (1955), no. 9, The Plymstock hoard.

Kendrick, T. D., The Hameldon Down Pommel. *Ant. J.* XVII (1937) p. 313.

Patchett, F. M., Cornish Bronze Age pottery. *Arch. J.* CI (1944) p. 29, CVII (1950) p. 49. Classes B and C for ribbon-handled urns.

Piggott, S., The early Bronze Age in Wessex. *P.P.S.* 1938, p. 52. The classic article defining the Wessex culture.

PIGGOTT, S., Bronze double-axes in the British Isles, *P.P.S.* (1953), p. 224.

RADFORD, C.A.R. and ROGERS, E.H., The excavations of two barrows at East Putford. *P.D.A.E.S.* III (1947) p. 156.

CHAPTER VI

APSIMON, A.M., Cornish Bronze Age pottery, *P.W.C.F.C.* II (1957 –1958) p. 36. The Trevisker, St Eval, series: the excavation report by E. Greenfield and A. ApSimon will be published by the Ministry of Works.

ASHBEE, P., *The Bronze Age round barrow in Britain* (1960).

BORLASE, W.C., Typical specimens of Cornish barrows. *Arch.* XLIX (1886) p. 181.

CHANTER, J.F., Examination of one of the Chapman barrow group. *T.D.A.* XXXVII (1905) p. 93.

CHRISTIE, P.A., Crig-a-Mennis: a Bronze Age barrow at Liskey, Perranzabuloe, Cornwall. *P.P.S.* 1960, p. 76.

FOX, A., Celtic fields and farms on Dartmoor. *P.P.S.* 1954, p. 87.

FOX, A., Excavations on Dean Moor, 1954–6. *T.D.A.* LXXXIX (1957) p. 18.

FOX, A., Excavations at Kestor. *T.D.A.* LXXXVI (1954) p. 21.

GODWIN, H., Prehistoric trackways of the Somerset level. *P.P.S.* (1960), p. 1.

GRAY, H. ST G., Excavations at Combe Beacon, Combe St Nicholas. *P. Som. A.S.* LXXXI (1935) p. 83.

GRAY, H ST. G., Double-looped palstave from Curland, Taunton. *Ant. J.* XVII (1937) p. 63. See also H.N. Savory *P.P.S.* 1949, p. 128.

HAWKES, C.F.C., The Towednack gold hoard. *Man.* (1932) no. 222, p. 177.

HAWKES, C.F.C. (editor), *Inventaria Archaeologica*. Great Britain. I (1955) No. 4, The Crediton hoard.

HODGES, H., The Bronze Age moulds of the British Isles. *Sibrium* V (1960) p. 153.

RADFORD, C.A.R., Prehistoric settlements on Dartmoor and the Cornish moors. *P.P.S.* 1952, p. 55.

ROGERS, E.H., The excavation of a barrow on Brownstone farm, Kingswear. *P.D.A.E.S.* III (1947) p. 164.

SHEPPERD, P.A., A Bronze Age cemetery at Porth Mellon, Meva-
gissey. *P.W.C.F.C.* II (1960–61) p. 197.
SMITH, M.A. (editor), *Inventaria Archaeologica,* Great Britain VII (1959).
Nos. 42–46. Monkswood, Taunton, Edington Burtle and Sparkford
ornament hoards.
SMITH, M.A., Some Somerset hoards and their place in the Bronze Age
of southern Britain. *P.P.S.* 1959, p. 144.
THOMAS, A.C., *Gwithian. Ten Years' work* 1949–58 (1958).
THOMAS, A.C., MEGAW, J.V.S., and WAILES, B., The Bronze Age
settlement at Gwithian, Cornwall. Preliminary report. *P.W.C.F.C.* II
(1960–61) p. 200.
WORTH, R.H., *Dartmoor* (1953). The Dartmoor hut circles p. 99. The
prehistoric pounds of Dartmoor p. 133. Summaries of the early excavations by the Dartmoor Exploration Committee of the Devonshire
Association.

CHAPTER VII

ALLEN, D.F., The Origins of Coinage in Britain, in *Problems of the
Iron Age* ed. S.S.Frere *Inst. of Arch.* occ. p., No. 11, (1961) p. 97.
Coins found in the south-west are in the gazetteer, p. 145: hoards,
p. 286.
ALLEN, D.F., The Paul (Penzance) hoard of imitation Massilia
drachms. *Num. Chron.* 7th ser. I, (1961), p. 91.
BATE, C.S., A British cemetery near Plymouth (Mount Batten) *Arch.*
XL (1871) p. 500, see also R.H.Worth *Trans. Plymouth Institution*
XVII (1931) p. 228.
BULLEID, A.H. and GRAY, H.ST G., *The Glastonbury lake village,* i and
ii (1911, 1917), *Meare lake village,* i and ii (1948, 1953).
COTTON,M.A., Cornish cliff-castles. *P.W.C.F.C.* II (1958–9) p. 113.
CRAWFORD, O.G.S., The ancient settlements at Harlyn Bay. *Ant. J.* I
(1927) p. 283.
CROFTS,C.B., Maen Castle, Sennen. *P.W.C.F.C.* I (1955) p. 98
DUDLEY, D., An excavation at Bodrifty, Mulfra, near Penzance. *Arch.
J.* CXIII (1956) p. 1.
DYMOND, C.W. and TOMKINS, H.G., *Worlebury* (1904).
FOX,A., An Iron Age bowl from Rose Ash, N. Devon. *Ant. J.* XLI
(1961) p. 186.

Fox, A., Two Greek silver coins from Holne, S. Devon. *Ant. J.* XXX (1950) p. 152.

Fox, A., Excavations at Kestor. *T.D.A.* LXXXVI (1954) p. 39. for iron-working.

Fox, A., Hill-slope forts and related earthworks in south-west England and South-Wales. *Arch. J.* CIX (1952) p. 1.

Fox, A., South-western hill-forts in *Problems of the Iron Age* ed. S. S. Frere *Inst. of Arch.* occ. p., No. 11, (1961) p. 35.

Fox, A., RADFORD, C. A. R. and SHORTER, A. H., Report on the excavations at Milber Down, 1937-8. *P.D.A.E.S.* IV (1949-50) p. 27.

Fox, SIR C., *Pattern and Purpose* (1958). The mirrors p. 84.

Fox, SIR C., Triskeles, palmettes and horse-brooches (the Polden hoard) *P.P.S.* 1952 p. 47.

GORDON, A. S. R., The excavation of Gurnard's Head, a cliff-castle in W. Cornwall. *Arch. J.* XCVII (1940) p. 96.

HAWKES, C. F. C., The A.B.C. of the British Iron Age, in *Problems of the Iron Age* ed. S. S. Frere, *Inst. of Arch.* occ. p., No. 11, (1961) p. 1. Sets out the current chronological scheme.

LEEDS, E. T., Excavations at Chun Castle, Penwith. *Arch.* 76 (1926-7) p. 205.

LIDDELL, D. M., Excavations at Hembury fort, Devon. *P.D.A.E.S.* I (1930) p. 40, (1931) p. 90, (1932) p. 162, II (1935) p. 135.

ORDNANCE SURVEY, *Map of Southern Britain in the Iron Age* (1962).

RADFORD, C. A. R., Report on the excavations at Castle Dore. *J.R.I.C.* new series I (1951) p. 1.

RICHARDSON, K. M. and YOUNG, A., Report on the excavations at Blackbury Castle. *P.D.A.E.S.* V (1954-5) p. 43.

SAUNDERS, A. D., Excavations at Castle Gotha, St Austell. Interim report. *P.W.C.F.C.* II (1960-61) p. 216.

THREIPLAND, L. M., An excavation at St Mawgan-in-Pyder, N. Cornwall. *Arch. J.* CXIII (1956) p. 33.

WILLIS, L. and ROGERS, E. H., Dainton earthworks. *P.D.A.E.S.* IV (1951) p. 79.

CHAPTER VIII

ANDREW, C. K. C., Trevelgue Head promontory fort, note, Roman Britain in 1939; *J.R.S.* XXX (1940) p. 175.

CLARKE, E.M., *Cornish fogous* (1962).

FOWLER, P.J., A native homestead of the Roman period at Porth Godrevy, Gwithian. *Cornish Archaeology* I (1962) p. 17.

Fox, A., *Roman Exeter* (1952) see also *ARCH. J.* CXIV (1957), Exeter meeting, p. 178 where references given to later work.

Fox, A., Roman objects from Cadbury Castle: *T.D.A.* LXXXIV (1952) p. 105.

Fox, A. and RAVENHILL, W.D., A Roman signal station on Stoke Hill, Exeter. *T.D.A.* XCI (1959) p. 71.

HAVERFIELD, F. and TAYLOR, M. V., Romano-British Cornwall. *V.C.H.* ii Part 5, (1924).

HENCKEN, H.O'N., Excavation at Chysauster, 1931. *Arch.* 83 (1933) p. 237.

HIRST, F. C., Excavations at Porthmeor 1933-5. *J.R.I.C.* XXIV (1936) p. 1.

MARGARY, I.D., *Roman Roads in Britain,* I (1955) p. 104–117.

RICHMOND, I.A., CRAWFORD, O.G.S. and WILLIAMS, I., The British section of the Ravenna Cosmography. *Arch.* 93 (1949) p. 1. The south-west, p. 17.

O'NEIL, B.ST J., The Roman villa at Magor farm, near Camborne, Cornwall. *J. Brit. Arch. Ass.* XXXIX (1933) p. 116.

ORDNANCE SURVEY, *Map of Roman Britain* (1956).

ST JOSEPH, H., Air Reconaissance in Britain (North Tawton fort). *J.R.S.* (1958), p. 98, see also *T.D.A.* XCI (1959) p. 174.

STEVENS, C.E., A lady of quality from Roman Devonshire. *T.D.A.* LXXXIV (1952) p. 172.

TAYLOR, M.V., The Sidmouth bronze, legionary standard or tripod. *Ant. J.* XXIV (1944) p. 22.

WEBSTER, G., The Roman advance under Ostorius Scapula. *Arch. J.* CXV (1958) p. 49.

WEBSTER, G., An excavation at Nunnington Park, Wiveliscombe, Somerset. *P. Som. A.S.* CIII (1958) p. 81.

WEDLAKE, W., *Excavation at Camerton, Somerset* (1958). The pewter industry, p. 82.

WOOLNER, A. and D., Teignbridge and the Haldon road. *T.D.A.* LXXXVI (1954) p. 211. and XCI (1959) p. 149.

CHAPTER IX

CHANTER, J.F., An inscribed stone between Parracombe and Lynton. *T.D.A.* XLV (1913) p. 270.

DOBLE, G.H., *The Saints of Cornwall,* in progress; Pt. 1. The Land's End district (1960). Pt. 2. The Lizard district (1962).

FOWLER, P.J. and THOMAS, A.C., Arable fields of the pre-Norman period at Gwithian. *Cornish Archaeology* I (1962) p. 61.

FOX, A., A. Dark Age trading site at Bantham, S. Devon. *Ant. J.* XXXV (1955) p. 55.

JACKSON, K., *Language and History in Early Britain* (1953) for the general background.

MACALISTER, R.A.S., *Corpus Inscriptionum Insularum Celticarum,* I (1945), Cornwall, Devon and Somerset, pp. 435–78.

NASH-WILLIAMS, V.E., *The early Christian Monuments of Wales* (1950).

ORDNANCE SURVEY, *Map of Britain in the Dark Ages* (1935).

RADFORD, C.A.R., Tintagel, the Castle and Celtic monastery, *Ant. J.* XV (1935) p. 401. *idem.* Tintagel in history and legend *J.R.I.C.* XXV (1942) p. 25.

RADFORD, C.A.R., Report on the excavations at Castle Dore. *J.R.I.C.* new series I (1951) p. 60.

RAVENHILL, W.D., Cornish Dark Age settlement, *Geography* XL (1955) p. 237. Settlement of Devon in the Dark Ages. *T.D.A.* LXXXVI (1954) p. 63.

THOMAS, A.C., Cornwall in the Dark Ages. *P.W.C.F.C.* II (1957–8) p. 59.

THOMAS, A.C., *Gwithian. Ten Years' work* 1949–58 (1958).

THOMAS, A.C., Imported pottery in Dark Age western Britain. *Med. Arch.* III (1959) p. 89.

Sources of Illustrations

The majority of the photographs have been specially taken for this book by Mr W. Hoskin, Exeter University photographer, in Exeter, Taunton and Truro Museums and in the field. Plates 7, 8, 42 and 90, the author.

The air-photographs, Plates 46, 47, 53, 65, 66, 69, 71, 72, 85, 86, and 92 are from the Cambridge University collection (curator Dr J. K. St Joseph) Crown copyright. Plate 70 was taken by Lt. C. S. Fox, R. N.

Plates 3, 4, 5, 6, 7, 22, 54, 55, 60, 67, 68, 93 are from the collection of Mr Charles Woolf, M. P. S., Newquay. Plates 24, 33, 34, 36, 51, 76, 78, 81, 82, 94, 96 and 97 are reproduced by permission of the Trustees of the British Museum. Plates 17, 18, 19, 54, 55 and 98 are reproduced by permission of the Ancient Monuments Branch of the Ministry of Public Buildings and Works and with the consent of Mr Paul Ashbee and Mrs. P. Christie. Plate 20 is reproduced by permission of Mr. D. P. Wilson; Plate 21, the Trustees of the late R. Hansford Worth; Plates 38 and 41, Plymouth City Museum; Plate 43 and 44, Mr Charles Thomas; Plates 48 and 49, the National Museum of Antiquities of Scotand; Plate 77, the City Museum Bristol; Plates 79 and 80, Professor Stuart Piggott; Plate 87, Exeter City Council; Plate 91, The Ashmolean, Oxford.

The co-operation of all these individuals and public bodies is gratefully acknowledged.

FIGURES   The maps have been redrawn mostly from my originals by Mr H. A. Shelley, Miss M. R. Bethell and Mr R. Fry. Fig. 43 is based on the Ordnance Survey's map of Roman Britain, Fig. 50 on Britain in the Dark Ages, both with minor modifications.

The original drawings, many based on work in the field, were drawn by Gillian Lamacraft (Figs. 4, 11, 13, 15, 17, 18, 19, 30, 33, 34, 35, 40, 47 and 48), Christine Wilkins (Figs. 8, 9, 12 and 26), Gillian Jones (Figs. 20 and 32), Rosemary Campbell (Fig. 16), and A. Clark (Fig. 23). Figures 4, 9, 13, 16, 17, 23, 25, 27, 28, 29, 38, 44, 45, 49 and 51 were redrawn at Thames & Hudson, for use in this book. Fig. 5 is reproduced by permission of Professor Stuart Piggott; Fig. 10, Bernard Wailes; Fig. 12, C. A. R. Radford; Fig. 15, Paul Ashbee; Fig. 35, Mrs P. Christie; Fig. 39, Mrs L. Murray-Threipland; Fig. 45, R. P. Wright; Fig. 48, Mrs E. V. Clark; Fig. 51, Charles Thomas, to all of whom grateful acknowledgement is made.

THE PLATES

1

2

3

4

6

12

13a

14

13b

13c

15

16

17

18

19

20

21

22

23

24

25

26

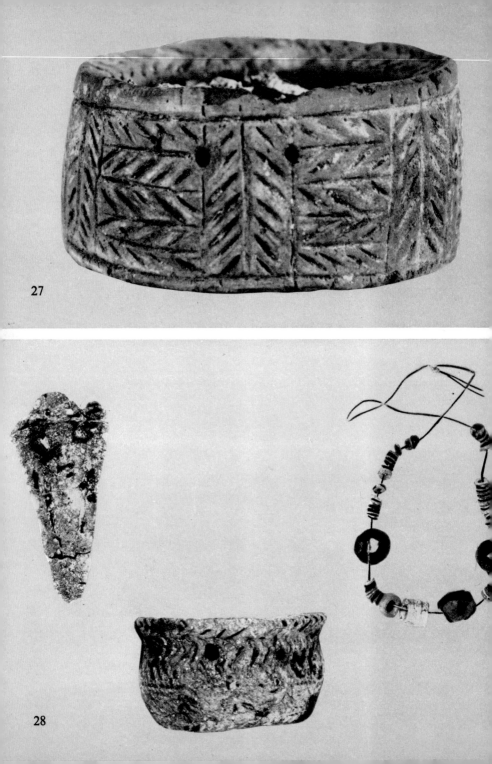

27

28

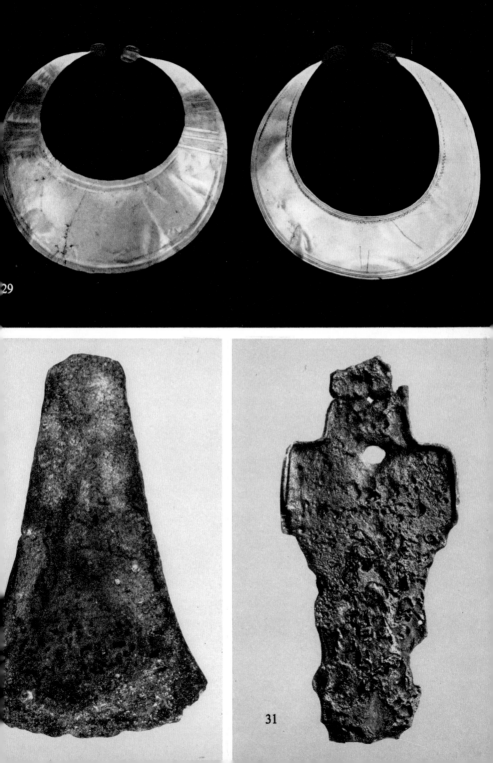

29

31

35

37

38

39

40

41

42

43

4

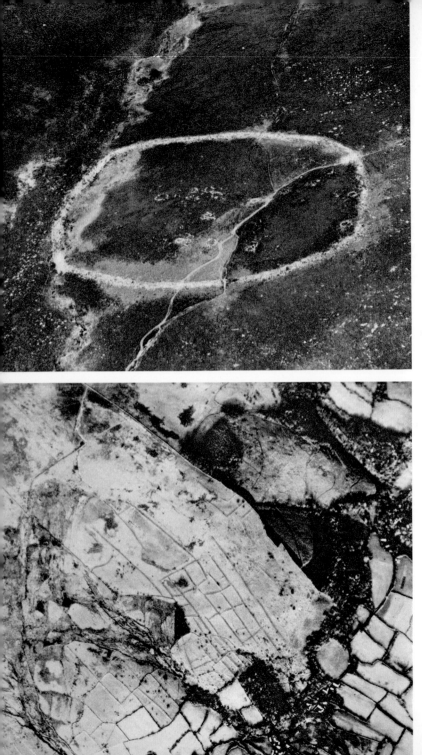

46

47

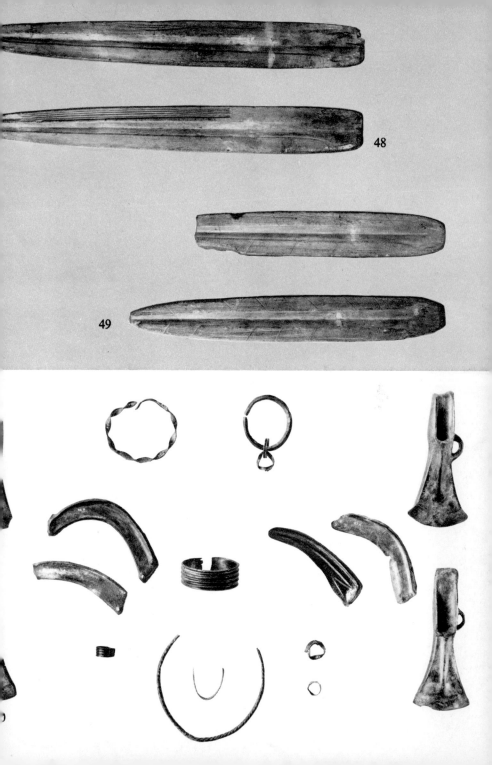

48

49

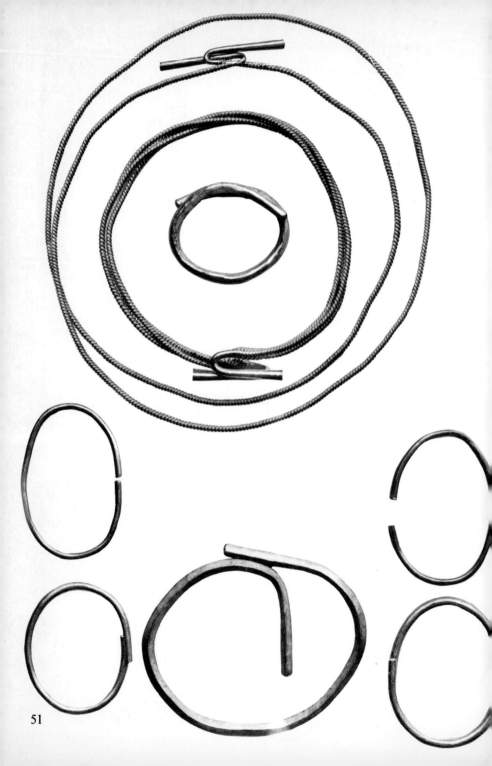

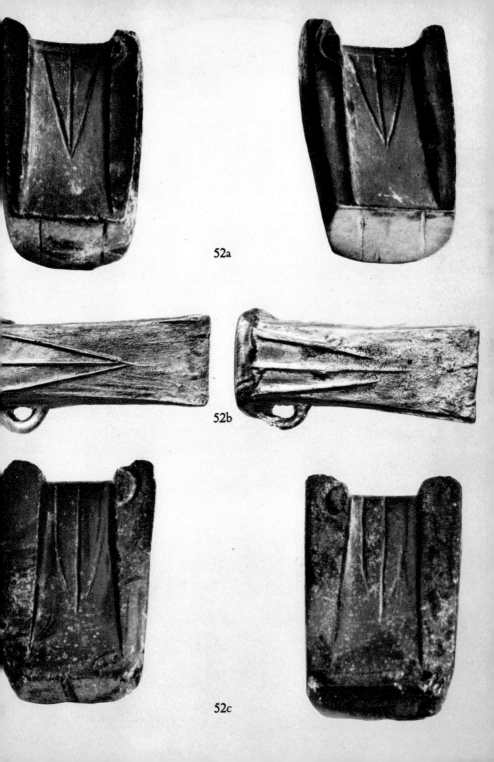

52a

52b

52c

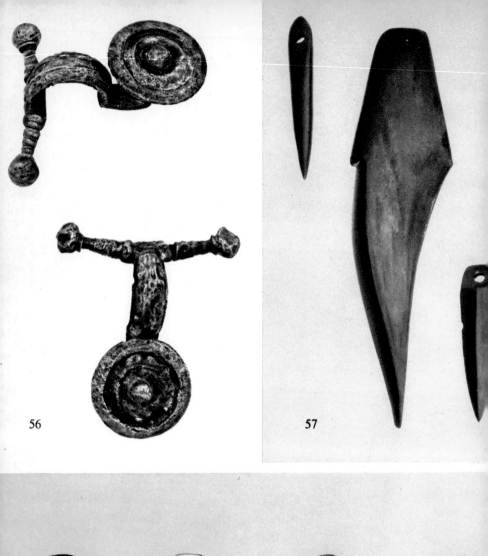

56

57

58

62

63

64

67

68

71

72

73

74

75

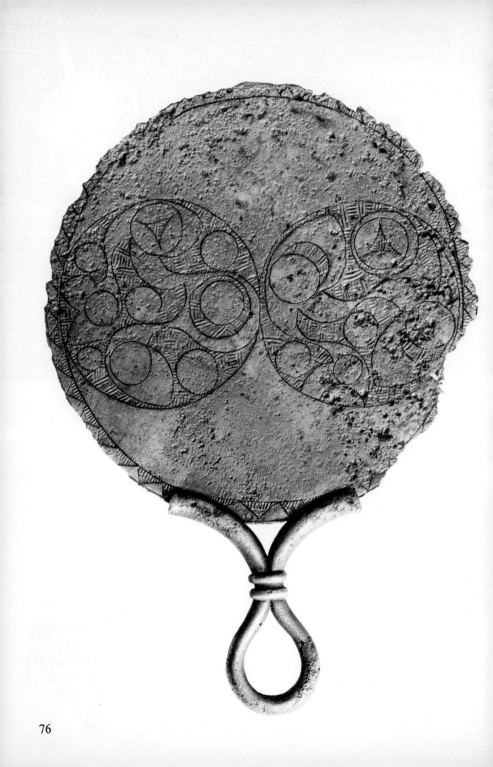

77   78

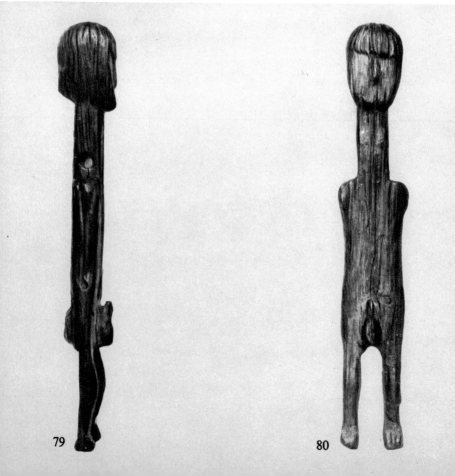

79   80

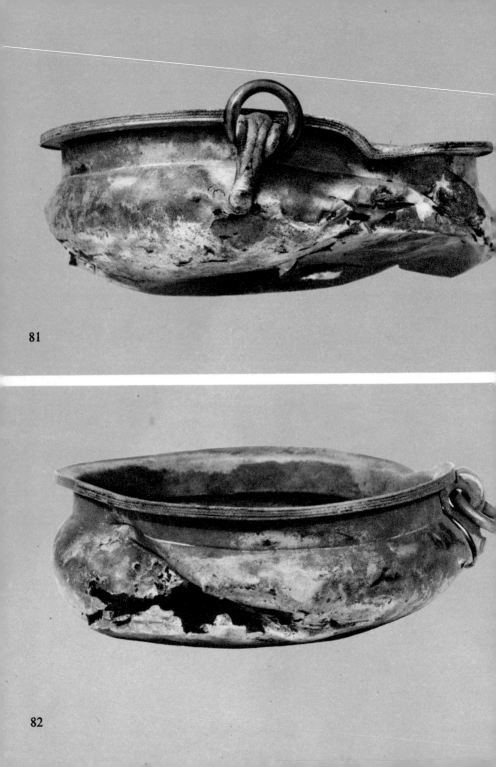

81

82

33

34

85

86

92

93

4

5

96

98

Notes on the Plates

2 Pottery bowls with horizontal lug handles from the early Neolithic causeway camp at Hembury, east Devon. No. 2 is in fine red ware with igneous grits and has the characteristic south-western trumpet lug. Height 6.8 and 4.8 in. Exeter Museum.

3 Chamber tomb at Pawton, Wadebridge, Cornwall. A broken piece of the capstone is on the left of the mound, in front of the façade of the closed chamber.

4 Neolithic henge monument at Castilly, Innis Down, Cornwall. The entrance is on the far side of the arena.

5 Zennor Quoit chamber tomb, Zennor, west Cornwall. The main chamber lies beneath the tilted capstone, the ante-chamber is behind the two upright stones of the façade.

6 Chamber tomb at Trethevy, St Clears, east Cornwall, from the south; the ante-chamber and tomb entrance face east.

7 Carn Gluze, St Just, west Cornwall: the central area. The primary pit of this ritual monument is in the middle surrounded by recent walling: the corbelled and domed cairn which covered it has been cleared of loose stones to show its original outline. Outside this is the cairn-ring which contained an Entrance Grave (Plate 8), retained by recent walling. The whole monument has now been cleared of undergrowth by the Ministry of Works.

8 Carn Gluze, St Just. The Entrance Grave on the circumference of the cairn-ring. Burnt human bones and potsherds were found below its floor when it was excavated by W. C. Borlase in 1874.

9   Three pottery cremation urns from Knackyboy Entrance Grave, St Martins, Scilly. These biconical urns have lug handles and were decorated with stitches and twists of thread or sinew impressed before firing. They came from the lower level in the tomb and were associated with glass and faience beads of the early Middle Bronze Age. Height 11, 10.6 and 11.4 in. Truro Museum.

10 Pottery cup with grooved decoration from the Neolithic settlement on Haldon, Devon. Height 4 in. Exeter Museum.

11 Entrance Grave at Pennance, Zennor, west Cornwall. The mound, which is edged with granite boulders, is 26 feet in diameter and 6 feet high.

12 Flint knife–dagger notched for hafting from the Wick Barrow, Somerset. Length 5.3 in. Taunton Museum.

13 Bell and long-necked beakers from the Wick barrow, Stogursey, Somerset, found with three inhumations which were approximately contemporary. The flint-knife dagger (12) was found with the necked beaker with chevron decoration (13a). The characteristic geometric ornament has been done with a toothed comb. Height 7 in., 6.3 in., and 6 in. Taunton Museum.

14 Necked beaker from Fernworthy, Devon. It was found with a bronze blade and a shale button with a V-perforation beneath a small cairn, associated with stone rows and a circle on Dartmoor. Height 6½ in. Plymouth Museum.

15 Handled beaker from Try, Gulval, Cornwall. It was found with cremated bones in a cist at the base of a standing stone or menhir. It is a late example, transitional to the early Bronze Age. Height 6.3 in. Truro Museum.

16 Food-vessel, southern type, from a primary cremation at Broad Down, Farway, east Devon. The broad rim indicates a late Neolithic (Peterborough) ancestry. Height 5 in. Exeter Museum.

7   Tregulland barrow, Wilsey Down, Cornwall. In the centre is the pit for the primary burial which had been disturbed, surrounded by the cairn, ring and stake circles. In the foreground are holes which contained ritual fires and a satellite grave for a cremation with arrowheads. The food,vessel, which dates the barrow to the Early Bronze Age, was found with a crema, tion inside the cairn,ring. In the background, a section of the covering mound and the ditch.

8   Flint arrowheads from the satellite grave in Tregulland barrow. The finely worked example with the hollow base for the insertion of the shaft has analogies in Brittany. Height $1\frac{1}{4}$ in. Truro Museum.

9   Cup,marked stone from the Tregulland barrow. It was placed over the satellite cremation grave. The pecked hollows and grooves are magical signs presumably to protect the dead. Length 7 in. Truro Museum.

0   Down Tor stone row and cairn, Sheepstor, Devon. The alignment is 1145 feet long and leads up to a low cairn edged with granite boulders and with a central cist. The tallest stone in the row is $9\frac{1}{2}$ feet high.

1   Stone rows at Shovel Down, Chagford, Devon. The double alignment is 380 feet long and 5 feet wide: it leads to a cairn on the crest of the ridge.

2   Stone circle at Tregaseal, St Just, Cornwall. In the background is Carn Kenidjack, a typical granite tor. Height of stones 3–4 feet, diameter 66 feet.

3   Scorhill stone circle, Gidleigh, Devon. Diameter 88 ft; tallest stone 8 ft.

4   Gold cup from Rillaton, Linkinhorne, east Cornwall. It was found in 1818 in a cist containing a secondary inhumation with other grave goods in a large barrow on Bodmin Moor. It was lost for many years but ultima, timately was re,discovered in the royal collections at Buckingham Palace and is now in the British Museum. The form is derived from gold corru, gated cups in the shaft graves at Mycenae. Height $3\frac{1}{4}$ in. British Museum.

6   Shale cups from the Early Bronze Age (Wessex) cemetery, Broad Down, Farway, Devon. The decorated example was associated with a primary

235

cremation, the plain one with a bronze grooved dagger and burnt bones. Height 3¾ in and 3¼ in. Exeter Museum.

27   Pottery pygmy cup from the Early Bronze Age (Wessex) cemetery, Broad Down, Farway, Devon. It contained the burnt bones of an infant. The twin perforations, *oculi*, and the incised decoration are a protective symbol, resembling a face. Height 1½ in. Exeter Museum.

28   Grave-goods from an Early Bronze Age cremation at Stevenstone farm, Upton Pyne, Exeter. The bronze dagger is grooved with two rivet holes, the pygmy pottery cup has eye-holes and twisted cord decoration, the necklace consists of three varieties of shale beads and a fossil encrinite. A much-corroded bronze pin which also came from this site (not illustrated) had a spiral stem. Length of dagger 3.8 in. Height of cup 1.3 in. Exeter Museum.

29, 30   Two gold lunulae found with a bronze flat axe (Plate 30) in a stone cist in 1865 at Harlyn Bay, St Merryn, Cornwall. Diameters 8.3 and 8.6 in. Length of flat axe 4.3 in. Truro Museum.

31   Bronze short sword from an Early Bronze Age cremation at Pelynt, south Cornwall. The squared flanges and rivet hole are for the attachment of the hilt. The weapon was imported from the Mediterranean in the thirteenth or twelfth century B.C. and like the double-axe from Topsham (Plate 34) is evidence of extensive trade movements. Length 4¼ in. Truro Museum.

32   Gold lunula from a bog on Cargurra farm, St Juliot, Cornwall. These crescentic necklaces of thin gold sheet with incised geometric patterns were imported from Ireland in the Early Bronze Age, probably in exchange for Cornish tin. Diameter 8 in. Truro Museum.

33   Amber pommel of a dagger from an Early Bronze Age barrow on Hameldon, Manaton, Devon. The pommel is decorated in *pointillé* technique with gold pins and has been repaired in antiquity. The original perished in the bombing of Plymouth in 1943 and our knowledge is derived from British Museum photographs taken in 1936. Diameter 2.3 by 1.3 in.

Double-axe of copper with oval shaft-hole from Mount Howe, Topsham, Devon. This prestige weapon was imported from the Aegean in the thirteenth century B.C. (*Cf.* Plate 31). Length 4.7 in. British Museum.

Necklace of shale, amber and faience beads from an Early Bronze Age cremation on Bamfylde Hill, North Molton, Devon. The blue segmented faience beads are of Egyptian origin and were imported in the fourteenth century B.C.: the two biconical faience beads in the centre of the necklace are unique in Britain but matched at Kerstrobel, Brittany. Exeter Museum.

Ribbon-handled urn from Tregaseal, St Just, Cornwall. It was found with a cremation in a cist contemporary with an Entrance-grave. The zig-zag and lozenge decoration is in plaited cord technique and there is a cross in relief on the base to strengthen it. A Middle Bronze south-west regional type (*Cf.* Plate 55). Height 20¼ in. British Museum.

Ribbon-handle and decorated rim of a pottery urn from Harlyn Bay, St Merryn, Cornwall. It was found with a cremation and bronze pins, since lost, in 1901. The decoration was made by impressing a plait of three thongs on the wet clay, producing a pattern resembling a laurel wreath or an ear of wheat. It is characteristic of the first phase of south-western Middle Bronze Age ceramics. Handle 3 in. wide. Truro Museum.

Pot from the Dewerstone, Dartmoor, found intact in a crevice by a rock-climber. The lug handles, grooved neck and row of depressions indicate a relationship with the Deverel-Rimbury urns of Dorset and also with that from Elworthy, Somerset, (Plate 40). Height 5.2 in. Plymouth Museum.

Two cremation urns from Knackyboy Entrance Grave, St Martins, Scilly. These came from the latest burials in the grave (*Cf.* Plate 9) and show the devolution of the biconical form and the development of incised decoration in the late Middle Bronze Age. That on the right can be related to the globular (Deverel-Rimbury) urns of southern England. Heights. 13¾ in. and 13 in. Truro Museum.

Cremation urn from Elworthy, Somerset, found in a cist within a 6 foot stone circle under a barrow. The incised decoration and paired dimples are characteristic of the late Middle Bronze Age. Height 9¼ in. Taunton Museum.

41 Storage pot from the enclosed settlement at Raddick Hill, Meavy, Dartmoor. It was found complete in a pit in a hut floor. The crude incised decoration and the heavy cordon and lugs are characteristic of late Middle Bronze Age ceramics in the south-west. Height 10½ in. Plymouth Museum.

42 Hut in an enclosed Bronze Age settlement at Dean Moor, South Brent, Dartmoor. Ranging poles and pegs indicate the entrance and the post-holes for the roof supports. Diameter 26 feet.

43 Plough-marks from the Bronze Age settlement at Gwithian, Hayle, Cornwall. The dark furrows were produced by cross-ploughing with an *ard* on light sandy soil.

44 Bronze Age spade-marks at Gwithian, made by a triangular blade, similar to the modern long-handled shovel. The impressions filled up with blown sand and so show as light marks.

45 Huts and field-walls at Kestor, Chagford, Devon. The large granite slabs used to line the hut walls are characteristic of late Bronze–early Iron Age settlements on eastern Dartmoor. Hut diameter 29 feet.

46 Grimspound enclosed settlement, Manaton, Dartmoor. It is sited in a dip between two tors at 1500 feet, at the head of the Grims Lake stream which runs through the enclosure. The massive granite wall is 10 feet thick with a single entrance and there are 24 small round huts inside. It was excavated in the late nineteenth century without result. A pastoral settlement, which although no sure evidence exists is probably of Middle to Late Bronze Age date.

47 Huts and fields on the slopes of Horridge Common, Ilsington, Dartmoor. The late Bronze–early Iron Age small square fields have been partly incorporated in a medieval strip field system.

48, 49 Stone moulds for bronze rapiers from the river Teign, Hennock, Devon.

The lower mould in Plate 48 has a matrix for a ribbed bracelet incorporated. The moulds in Plate 49 have diagonal casting vents on the margins. Originals lost; photographed from casts in the National Museum of Antiquities, Edinburgh. Lengths 24½ and 21½ in.

Middle Bronze Age 'ornament hoard' from Edington Burtle, Somerset. The objects were buried in a wooden box and are a metal-worker's stock-in-trade: they comprise four high-flanged palstaves of south-western type, four knobbed sickles, one of which (left) is unfinished, two twisted torcs, three bracelets and three finger rings. Length of palstaves 6 in., sickles 5¼ in. Taunton Museum.

Middle Bronze Age hoard of two gold twisted torcs and four bracelets from Towednack, Lelant, Cornwall. The two coiled bars of gold are ingots ready for manufacture of similar ornaments. The hoard which was buried in a field-bank of an ancient settlement probably belonged to a travelling Irish smith. Diameter of small torc 4½ in. the large torc is 45 in. long. British Museum

Stone moulds (*a* and *c*) for casting bronze three-ribbed looped and socketed axes from Helsbury, Cornwall. Length 4¾ and 5 in. Truro Museum. Cast of axes from the Helsbury moulds (52b). This type with heavily moulded socket and three ribs is peculiar to the south-west and south Wales in the late Bronze Age. Truro Museum.

Bronze Age barrows on the Taphouse ridge, Braddock, Cornwall. The ditch of a ploughed-out mound shows as a white circle in the distant pasture field.

Crig-a-Mennis ritual barrow, Perranzabuloe, Cornwall. In the centre is a cairn covering a deposit of charcoal, surrounded by the remains of a cairn-ring: in the foreground is the ditch with causeway entrance.

Ribbon-handled urns and miniature cup from Crig-a-Mennis barrow. The urns were buried separately in pits on the floor of the barrow without any signs of an interment. The urn on the left is decorated with plaited cord, that on the right with twisted cord; they date from the Middle Bronze Age. Height 14 in., 15½ in., 2½ in. Truro Museum.

56 Bronze brooches, La Tène I type, from Harlyn Bay, St Merryn, Cornwall found in slate-lined graves in the Early Iron Age inhumation cemetery. This form with a disc on the up-turned foot has Iberian affinities. Length, 1.3 in. Truro Museum.

57 Slate needles and a borer from the midden at the Early Iron Age settlement at Harlyn Bay, St Merryn, Cornwall. These are made from beach pebbles and are typical of a skilled local industry. Length 2.3, 2.6 and 6.3 in. Truro Museum.

58, 59 Greek silver coins from Holne, Devon. Plate 58, a tetradrachm of Alexander III of Macedon, issued after 326 B.C. Plate 59, a tetradrachm of Aesillas, Roman quaestor in Macedonia, issued 93–92 B.C. The coins are evidence for Mediterranean trade in the Iron Age. Actual size. Torquay Museum.

60 Tin ingot, dredged from the Fal estuary, St Mawes, Cornwall. The H shape, likened to an astragalus or knuckle-bone by Diodorus Siculus, would facilitate handling and transport. This ingot is tangible evidence for the export of Cornish tin in the Iron Age, and corroborates the classical writers' account. Length 2 feet 10 in. Weight 158 lbs. Truro Museum.

61 Three pots from Castle Dore hill-fort, Golant, Cornwall (Plate 69). The bold curvilinear and hatched decoration is characteristic of south-western ceramic in the Iron Age (South-Western Third B culture). Height $4\frac{1}{2}$, $12\frac{1}{4}$ and $7\frac{1}{2}$ in. Truro Museum.

62, 63 Bowl and pot from Meare lake-village, Somerset. The finely incised elaborate scroll patterns, roundels, cross-hatching and linear shading are characteristic of the Somerset school of potters in the second–first centuries B.C. Height $4\frac{3}{4}$ and 13.7 in. Taunton Museum.

64 Pot from Caerloggas, St Mawgan-in-Pyder, Cornwall. This came from the early levels in the hill-fort. Height 7 in. Truro Museum.

65 Dumpdon hill-fort, Luppitt, east Devon. The defences consist of a rampart, ditch and counterscarp bank on the steep sides of the hill, and

two widely spaced ramparts across the level approach. The fort has a deep in-turned entrance.

5 Hembury hill-fort, Payhembury, east Devon. The end of the spur is fortified by triple ramparts and ditches, downbuilt on the slopes and upcast across the spur, where the outer ditch is unfinished. There are two lateral entrances. The fort was occupied by South-Western Iron Age B peoples in the second and first century B.C. In the Late Iron Age there was a cultural change (*Cf.* Plate 75) and the interior was divided by two transverse banks and ditches across the centre of the fort.

8 Trevelgue promontory fort, Newquay, Cornwall. Above, the promontory from the north; below, the main defences across the narrowest part of the headland with an earlier (?) rampart behind.

9 Castle Dore hill-fort, Golant, Cornwall: a south-western regional type with a dependent enclosure.

0 Prestonbury hill-fort, Drewsteignton, Devon. A multiple-enclosure fort of south-western type above the Teign valley: it is defended on the east by an outer rampart or cross-bank with its ends resting on the steep scarps.

1 Clovelly Dykes hill-fort, Clovelly, north Devon. A concentric multiple-enclosure fort of two periods: the three strip-like enclosures on the right and the semicircular enclosure on the left are additions to the two original central enclosures. The main entrance to the outworks is in the foreground. The extent and multiplicity of the earthworks indicate that cattle-keeping was the principal occupation of the Iron Age inhabitants.

2 Resugga hill-fort, St Stephen-in-Brannel, Cornwall, a variant of the regional type, perhaps unfinished. The main enclosure is on level ground backed by a fall to the valley. It is approached by a deeply worn embanked track, passing through two short lengths of rampart, unconnected with the inner enclosure. The hedge to the right is of recent date.

3 Glass beads from Meare lake-village, Somerset. The beads are of clear glass with spiral, chevron and rectangular patterns inlaid with chrome-yellow glass threads. Actual size. Taunton Museum.

74 Cordoned pot from Sennen, Land's End, Cornwall, an example of Late Iron Age ceramic (South-western third C). Height 6 in. Truro Museum.

75 Ribbed bead-rim bowl from Hembury hill-fort, east Devon (Plate 66). It came from the ditch silt of the transverse banks sub-dividing the fort and is typical of late Iron Age ceramic in east Devon and Dorset (Southern Third C). Height 3¾ in. Exeter Museum.

76 Bronze mirror from a woman's grave in the Trelan Bahow cemetery, St Keverne, Cornwall. The incised decoration with infilling of cross-hatching is characteristic of the south-western Celtic metal-workers. The designs on the paired roundels are abstract and asymmetrical. Probably mid-first century B.C. Height with handle, 6 in. British Museum.

77 Bronze collar from Wraxall, north Somerset. The two pieces are attached with a swivel joint at the back and fasten below the enlarged terminals with a mortise and tenon. The florid relief decoration of symmetrical hooked and running scrolls originally had insets of glass or enamel. Probably late first century B.C. Diameter 7 in. Bristol Museum.

78 Bronze collar from Trenoweth, Lelant, Cornwall. It is made of thin sheet bronze attached to a core of lead: the fastening of the two pieces is uncertain. The symmetrical stippled design retains some insets of clear and yellow glass. Probably early first century A.D. Diameter 6 in. British Museum.

79, 80 Wooden idol of oak, Teigngrace, Devon. It was found in 1866 in digging fireclay on the floor of the lower Teign valley, lying beside a tree-trunk under 25 feet of alluvial gravel. The hole in the neck was probably for the attachment of arms: the stylised treatment of the face and hair suggests a Celtic image of a fertility god. Height. 13.3 in. Watts, Blake, Bearne and Co., Zitherixon Clay Works, Newton Abbot.

81, 82 Bronze bowl from Munson farm, Rose Ash, north Devon, found whilst draining a bog. The bowl is paper-thin, hammered out and the rim finished by lathe turning. The escutcheon is a stylised animal-head, probably an ox. The wavy line punched on the rim is characteristic of south-western Celtic metal work. Late first century B.C.–A.D. Diameter 7½ in. British Museum.

4   Bronze bowl from Higher Youlton farm, Warbstow, Cornwall, found whilst draining a bog. The bowl is practically identical with that from Rose Ash and must be from the same south-western workshop. The escutcheon, shown inverted, is probably a grinning demon or grotesque human head, wearing a plumed helmet. Diameter 7¾ in. Truro Museum.

5   Old Burrow Roman fortlet, Countisbury, north Devon. The entrance to the inner enclosure is on the right, facing the coast. Excavations in 1963 showed that this outpost was occupied temporarily by Roman troops *circa* A.D. 50. Their function was to keep watch on the Silures across the Bristol Channel and signal to the fleet. Diameter of inner enclosure 90 feet.

6   Roman signal station on Stoke Hill, Exeter. The ditches in the air-photograph show as dark marks. The few finds from excavations in 1958–59 indicate it was occupied at the end of the third century A.D. It presumably was designed to give warning of sea raiders entering the Exe estuary to the citizens of *Isca Dumnoniorum* (Exeter).

7   The Roman city wall, inner by-pass (James Street), Exeter. The ashlar facing and chamfered plinth are of Trap, a local igneous rock and the core is of grouted rubble, pitched herring-bone fashion. There was a mid-second century rampart behind the wall in which modern cellars have been inserted. The wall was built by the citizens of *Isca Dumnoniorum circa* A.D. 200.

8   Bronze tripod mount from the beach at Sidmouth. It shows young Achilles riding Cheiron the centaur, who is teaching him to hunt an attacking wild beast. The mount ornamented the top of the leg of a folding tripod used to support a bronze wine bowl or table-tray. Probably second century A.D. Height 7 in. Exeter Museum.

9   Glass cup, handle missing, and bowl from Fore Street, Exeter, found in a refuse pit dating *circa* A.D. 55–75. The shape of the ribbed cup is derived from contemporary Roman silver. These vessels of bluish-green

glass were imported from Gaul or Germany in the first century A.D. Height 4½ and 2½ in. Exeter Museum.

90 Roman milestone, Mynheer farm, Gwennap Pit, Cornwall. The inscription reads IMP. CAES. ANT. GORDIANO PIO FEL and attests the repair or making of a road in west Cornwall in the reign of Gordian III, A.D. 238–240. Height 3 feet 7 in.

91 Finds from a well in a rectangular earthwork at Bosence, St Erth, Cornwall. The stone steel-yard weights are of granite, the jug and bowl of pewter: the bowl has a dedication to Mars by Aelius Modestus on the interior. The pewter vessels probably date from the fourth century A.D. and may have come from a nearby shrine. Height of jug 10½ in, diameter of bowl 4½ in. Ashmolean Museum.

92 Romano-British settlement at Chysauster, Gulval, Cornwall. The court-yard houses are aligned along a street: beside them are paddocks or garden plots, and in the foreground there are remains of lynchetted fields. The courtyard house is a native development confined to the Land's End peninsula.

93 Fogou at Carn Euny native settlement, Sancreed, Cornwall. This sub-terranean stone-lined passage with open ends connects with a large domed side-chamber, associated with a courtyard house; it was probably a communal cellar. Souterrains of this type are a native development confined to west Cornwall in the Late Iron Age and Roman period and are occasionally found built within small earthworks.

94 Pewter cup from Halviggan, St Stephen in Brannel, Cornwall. It was found in a tin stream in 1793; probably fourth century A.D. Height 4½ in. British Museum.

95 Memorial stone from Winsford Hill, west Somerset. The inscription in debased Roman capitals with ligatures reads CARATACI NEPUS, grandson of Caratacus. It was erected on the ridgeway on the crest of Winsford Hill, Exmoor, probably in the fifth or early sixth centuries A.D. Height 4 feet. Cast, Taunton Museum.

7 Memorial stone from Fardel, Ivybridge, south Devon. The edges of the stone have an Ogam Celtic inscription, SVAQQVCI MAQI (son of) QICI; on the face is the inscription in mixed Roman capitals and cursive of FANONI MAQVI RINI, dating from the sixth century; on the reverse the memorial of a third individual, SAGRANVI, in mixed capitals and uncial script, dating from the early seventh century. All three names are of Irish (Goidelic) origin. Height 5 feet 6 in. British Museum.

8 Tintagel Celtic monastery, Cornwall. The site on a cliff-ringed promontory was chosen by the monks for its wildness and remoteness. The chapel, cells and main monastic buildings were on the top of the headland; those illustrated in a relatively sheltered position on the north-east side include the scriptorium.

Index

(S) indicates that the site is in Somerset; (D), in Devon; (C), in Cornwall

Index